ORGANIZE YOUR WAY

Simple Strategies for Every Personality

Katie McMenamin and Kelly McMenamin

Founders of PixiesDidIt!®

Illustrations by

Carol Breckenridge of BreckWorks

An Imprint of Sterling Publishing Co., Inc.
1166 Avenue of the Americas
New York, NY 10036

STERLING and the distinctive Sterling logo are registered trademarks
of Sterling Publishing Co., Inc.

ISBN 978-1-4549-2035-9

Distributed in Canada by Sterling Publishing Co., Inc.
c/o Canadian Manda Group, 664 Annette Street
Toronto, Ontario, Canada M6S 2C8
Distributed in the United Kingdom by GMC Distribution Services
Castle Place, 166 High Street, Lewes, East Sussex, England BN7 1XU
Distributed in Australia by NewSouth Books
45 Beach Street, Coogee, NSW 2034, Australia

For information about custom editions, special sales, and premium and corporate purchases, please contact Sterling Special Sales at 800-805-5489 or specialsales@sterlingpublishing.com.

Manufactured in Canada

2 4 6 8 10 9 7 5 3 1

www.sterlingpublishing.com

Design by Chris Thompson

Mom & Dad

For always encouraging us to follow our dreams and, in the words of Winston Churchill, "Never, never, in nothing great or small, large or petty—never give in except to convictions of honor and good sense."

Grandma Mc & Grandma B

For our two organizationally, diametrically opposed grandmothers, Maxine and Dorothy.

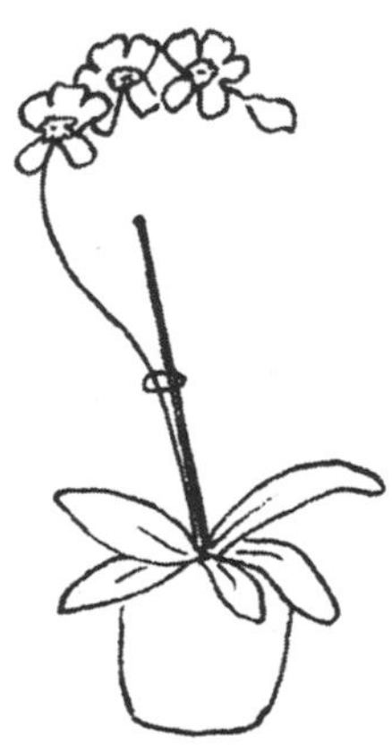

Contents

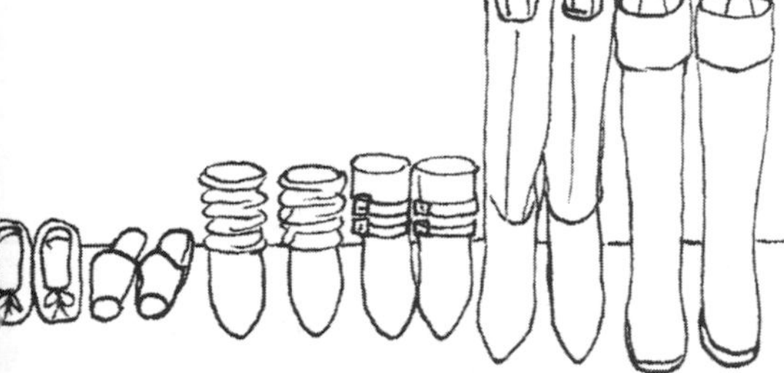

PROLOGUE

She said, *she* said: There are things to do, places to be— Maybe there's a good show on TV

You've bought the organizing files, boxes, shelves, and bins, but your house is still a mess. It's not you; it's the well-meaning people who think they know how you should be organized with a system that they claim will make your home look like one of those perfectly staged renovations on HGTV® or DIY Network®. Their systems do work, but not for everyone. That's because every brain is wired differently and has a unique way of coping and thriving in your house. And that's where personality theory comes in.

This book and our business, PixiesDidIt!®, are the result of: thirty-five–plus years of figuring out how to understand and respect each other's differences; more than two decades of studying personality type theory; and ten years of organizing the homes and offices of a wide range of clients, from multimillionaires with household help and endless piles of paper, to neatnik financiers with messy closets, to stay-at-home moms trying to keep ahead of toys that multiply like bunnies. Here's what we found: organization isn't one-size-fits-all. The same organizational advice is easy to follow for some clients and impossible for others. The trick is customizing that advice to your individual personality.

We know our solutions work because we get repeat customers—but never to readdress the same organizational dilemma. We build our solutions around our seven key principles and the strengths and weaknesses associated with each client's personality. One of our first questions to our clients is: How do you get organized on your own? That simple question can yield a lot of insight and help us tailor our system to the way your brain is wired.

We are sisters as different as Oscar and Felix of that classic 1970s TV series, *The Odd Couple*. Kelly makes her bed every morning. Katie does it when she's feeling the need for a fresh start. Kelly tidies her home every night and prepares coffee for the morning ahead. Katie cleans up when it's bugging her or she's expecting company. Kelly has daily To-Do checklists. Katie does 'em when she's feeling overwhelmed. Kelly has regular routines she rarely breaks. Katie has a few . . . off and on.

It's a miracle that we are on speaking terms, let alone business partners and best friends. Sharing a bedroom as children created some spectacular profanity-laden fights, but it also helped us develop a deep friendship. It was our dad who helped us see that our conflicts were innate, based on the way our brains were wired. Bored at a cocktail party, he wandered off and found a book about personality types that described his unique and eccentric personality to a tee. From thereon, personality type theory gave our family a way to understand why we often annoyed each other—and how to find a middle ground so we could get along. (Well, some of the time, anyway. . . .)

So, how did PixiesDidIt! come about? In 2002, Kelly was working as a research analyst at a hedge fund, and Katie was a stay-at-home mom, working on her novel, trying and failing to keep her busy home organized. Our parents have long referred to us as "The Pixies"—probably because our frequent squabbles, mischief, and gossip-laden banter reminded them of naughty Tinker Bell—so, with that moniker in mind, Katie said to Kelly, "Hey, when you're ready to quit the rat race, we can start a business together and—whatever we do—we can call it 'PixiesDidIt'!"

Kelly thought, "Are you crazy?!"

But life has a way of screwing up the perfect plans of even the most naturally organized among us: lo and behold, by 2006, Kelly grew tired of the hedge-fund world, Katie happily shelved the novel she was working on, and our organizing business was born. Before long, we discovered that clients with similar personality types tend to have the same organizational likes, dislikes, hang-ups, and visions. Our hunch was right.

At its core, organization is about retrieval: Can you find what you're looking for when you need it? That's it. Being organized doesn't mean your house is immaculate with nothing askew. When it comes down to it—even if some people think you don't *look* organized—if you can easily retrieve what you need, then you're organized. One personality type's idea of beauty or sentimentality is another's idea of clutter or mess. There is almost never one best way to organize an entryway or fold shirts or get rid of possessions. But there is one best way that works for *you*. Stick with what works. Or, as we say to our clients, "If it ain't broke, don't fix it."

We dispel the usual advice of almost every organizational guru. Spontaneous, non-bed-making paper pilers of the world like Katie, who have been put upon by schedule-happy, purge-obsessed neat freaks like Kelly, do not need to change who they are. Instead, we reveal how to organize your home according to your own unique personality and behavioral tendencies. Different people need different solutions. Your organizational system might not work for anyone else, but it will free you of clutter, guilt, and stress.

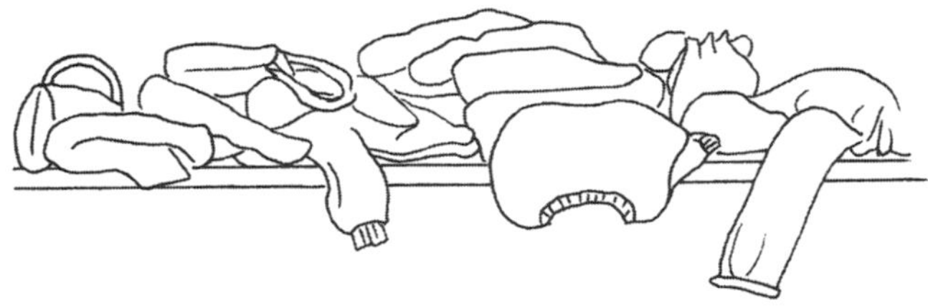

INTRODUCTION

Life should be easy. . . . (We know it isn't, but organizing it should be!)

Being disorganized sucks, and it's stressful—anyone searching for their keys when they're running late knows this. This occurrence is familiar to many of us, and it's why home organization is a growing industry with television channels dedicated to it, not to mention magazines, books, and entire stores. What's worse is that so many of us live and work with our organizational opposites, those who constantly tell us that we need to organize this way or that.

This book is a road map to understanding yourself, your organizational style, and the organizational style of the people you live with. It's about giving different people different solutions for the same organizational dilemmas. For instance, if you're visual, it will be easier for you to remember to pay your bills if they're laid out in a pile versus hidden in a drawer. Our advice is expansive but distilled down to seven nuggets of Pixie gold. Kelly puts them in numbered format because her personality type *loves* numbered lists:

1. Know and accept who you are.
2. Purge it your way.
3. Formalize your natural organizational tendencies.
4. It's all about retrieval.
5. Reduce organization procedures to as close to one step as possible.
6. Proudly use unconventional organizational solutions if they work for you.
7. Accept that there isn't one best organizational solution to every problem.

Keep these seven principles in mind whenever you're trying to create a new organizational system or solve an organizational problem. We want to share our "PixieDust" with the world, because being organized can change your life. The small amount of daily happiness you get from seeing all your clothes hung up in a neat row, the profound confidence that comes from knowing where things are, or the joy of retrieving a certain bag from a closet without having something fall on your head—it's life-changing. Being organized means you're managing your life; it's not managing you.

Know and accept who you are

This is the personality part. The first step is to figure out who you are. Take the PixieQuiz in Chapter 3 (page 19). Then read the description associated with your PixieType. If it fits like a glove, with perhaps just a few minor quibbles, you're almost done with this part. If your results don't resonate, scan a few other personality-type descriptions and see if one of those fits you better. The quiz results are not as important as identifying with the description. Why? Whether it's a quick fun quiz like ours or a more serious, psychometrically tested instrument, we all can provide answers that reflect our self-image but not our actual behavior.

Once you decide which description fits you best, the second step is to accept it. This is our first bit of "PixieDust": be honest with yourself and accept that you are who you are. This is difficult for some people. If you're "organizationally challenged" like Katie, you might be reluctant to accept that you're never going to be able to keep a To-Do list and check things off in a timely manner. As she says, "If we just try enough, find enough time, or get off the couch, we're convinced that we're going to be able to have a magazine-perfect home." But remember—and this is for *all* personality types—magazine perfection is styled by a professional. Even Oprah's closet doesn't look the way it does in her magazine. (Okay, maybe Oprah's does, but Oprah is Oprah®.) Plus, we bet she's got staff to maintain that perfection, and if you've bought a book to get yourself organized, we're betting you might be a little short on the household help. Therefore, for the Katies of the world, accept that perhaps your personality type is going to have a harder time creating magazine-level perfection than others. Let go. So what if you'd rather relax after a hard day than clean your kitchen? We've got solutions that will make it good enough.

Now, are you the type who's always making excuses for how tidy you are? Apologizing for your "OCD" habits? Enough, already! No shame and no blame! So you can't relax until your countertops are shining or the dishwasher's humming? *Big deal.* Unless you are obsessively washing your countertops until your hands are chapped, there is absolutely nothing wrong with you. Accept that you're always going to have to tidy up the house. It's not a personality disorder; it's your personality *type.* We've got solutions to make your life easier, because it's a heck of a lot of work being you—unless you have Oprah-level cash.

Purge it your way

We both thought we were brilliant coming up with this succinct way of describing our advice to clients until we realized it sounded awfully close to Burger King's old Have It Your Way® slogan, and we were not geniuses but rather dutiful TV watchers unable to fast-forward through commercials in the 1980s. That being said, half to three quarters of the pushback we get from people when it comes to organizing is about purging. When we first started out, we told people to only keep things that made them happy, are beautiful, or are very useful. Great advice. But *every* organizer tells you these things. We found that we are most helpful when we educate our clients about what makes purging difficult for them, so they can climb that wall if/when they hit it. It's our aim to do so in these pages as well. Every personality type needs the right impetus to throw stuff out, and we can show you what impetus works best for your type, as well as what fears lurk behind your decisions to keep things others might consider junk.

Most of us who have trouble getting rid of stuff have an irrational but real fear of not having enough. *So yeah, I have a dozen matching, reusable grocery bags, but I'm probably going to need a few plastic bags from the drugstore just in case. . . .* It's most likely the effect of being raised by people who lived through the last century's Great Depression, or maybe this century's Great Recession. When the economy is good, we accumulate stuff like squirrels, and then when times are tough, we have a hard time throwing away this useless stuff. Remember, getting rid of things is free, and the resulting empty and easier-to-organize space is one of the most freeing feelings in the world. Take the weight off already.

Formalize your natural organizational tendencies

Many people don't realize that in a world awash in images of magazine-perfect homes and preconceived notions about how everyone *should* organize, you're probably more organized than you think. If you know where things are when you need them and can keep it that way, then you are organized, regardless of how it looks or what people say. For example, someone filing away a "messy" person's piles without permission will soon discover that those massive piles were actually intricate, carefully designed, organizational holding pens. Conversely, an otherwise immaculate home might have fifteen canvas tote bags, stuffed on a shelf, that fall out of the front-hall closet whenever someone tries to retrieve one. Knowing where things are, easily retrieving them, and being able to maintain that system are the three essential building blocks to organization. Appearance doesn't matter as much as method—and matching it to the right person. The essence of who you truly are needs to determine *how* you organize—that's the PixieMagic!

Our second sprinkling of "PixieDust" is to take your working organizational systems and make them look and work better. Do you tend to have a lot of piles around your home office area but know where everything is? Then go out and get a bunch of matching translucent bins and contain those piles. All of a sudden your piles will *look* intentional and organized, and you'll feel better as a result. You'll also be a few steps closer to that magazine perfection we're all subconsciously aiming toward. If you're someone who just has a pile of mail on the counter in the kitchen, then go ahead and get an inbox already. Our PixieType personality descriptions will let you know if you're a piler or a filer, whether you need a bunch of matching bins or simply one catchall container. Or maybe you're the one with fifteen tote bags in your closet. Mount seven or eight hooks on the back of the door so there are only two bags on each hook (easy retrieval), or put up shelf dividers and place two bags in each slot. Formalize and create structure around the things you already do naturally. By doing so, you will look *and* feel more organized.

It's all about retrieval

Being organized means you can easily find things. It's *that* simple. Your house could look positively clinical with nary a crumb, but if you can't locate a Phillips-head screwdriver, an extra toothbrush, or your kid's permission slip for the field trip, then it's not working for you. The basic aim of organization is to know where things are and to be able to *retrieve* these things with minimal to no fuss. Every time you create a new home for something, ask yourself how hard or easy it will be to retrieve it. Your answer always lies in how much time and how many steps it takes to get it.

Reduce organization procedures to as close to one step as possible

Remember how many steps Mister Rogers took to take off his jacket, put on his sweater, take off his shoes, and put on his slippers? Oh, man, it takes a *lot* of patience to watch him, let alone do it yourself. Only Mister Rogers has that kind of time on his hands. No matter your personality, keep the retrieval as close to one step as possible. Remove your clothes-hamper lid if you leave dirty clothes on the floor or on top of an unused Exercycle® (and yes, get rid of the unused Exercycle already). If you've got kids, give them hooks at their height to hang up their coats. If you're an avid cook, keep your most-used spices and utensils on a lazy Susan next to the stove. You get the drift. No matter what your type, no matter what the task: the fewer the steps, the easier it is to maintain an organized home.

Proudly use unconventional organizational solutions if they work for you

Right now, Katie's hand is covered in a list of things she needs to do and can't forget. Yes, her *hand*. She's not the type to keep lists, but when she's got a lot of things on her plate, she has to start writing them down. When she doesn't have any room on her plate—e.g., start of the school year, three trips to NYC in two months, a book that needs to be written in six months—her right hand becomes that red string around her finger. (Yes, of course she's left-handed.) It's the definition of unconventional, but it works for her and that's what matters. (Before you dismiss us, note that billionaire Richard Branson unapologetically does the same thing when he hears a good idea he wants to remember but doesn't have his notebook on him.) If it works, do it.

Accept that there isn't one best organizational solution to every problem

From what we've observed over a lifetime of knowing each other and the last ten years of working with clients of all sorts of personality types, there is never going to be one "right" way to organize. Each organizational dilemma is going to present its own specific sets of problems that demand a unique solution, depending on space, money, and the personality types of those involved in maintaining it. Some of us are never going to hang up our coats on hangers like Mr. Rogers—even some "neat" types have difficulty doing so because that's not how they were raised—and some of us are always going to have to do the dishes before we go to bed. There isn't one best solution—just the best one for you.

Our motto is Life Should Be Easy® for a reason: we want you to be more organized, less stressed, and happier without having to change who you are. Our seven nuggets of "PixieDust" will help you do this. We don't all have Oprah's staff, but by following our advice you can get a lot closer to the ideal they promote on your own. We break down organization by room and then by personality type, so it's like a customized organizing resource or a "choose your own adventure" book! Once you know and accept your personality, you can go to your pages or check out why your wife is driving you crazy. We also include line-art illustrations with our advice, so you can "see" what we're talking about. Who doesn't love makeover "before and after" pictures? Our room-by-room approach will also help you learn to take organizing one step at a time, because getting organized always feels like a gargantuan project and everyone tends to put it off, no matter what their type.

We set up the structure of our book so we could explore every organizational hurdle in the home, from entryways and kitchens to organizing paper and decluttering rooms, to—the biggest part of our job—resolving organizational strife between different personality types! By addressing the personality conflicts with the people who share living space with you and your stuff, we have created an organizational system for keeping the stuff *and* keeping the peace!

Every chapter starts with what we call "universal solutions"—basic building blocks for all types upon which to build your own unique organizing systems—and ends with personality-specific advice. We reinforce our advice with personal anecdotes and PixieTips that highlight unconventional ideas and important considerations. And at the end of each chapter, we feature a checklist for religious list-making types to mark their headway and for everyone to celebrate how far they've come. We also have a resource section with recommended products for each personality type and for each space in your home (page 236). To communicate with us directly, visit our website (www.pixiesdidit.com) and get a virtual consultation, submit queries to our advice column, "Dear Katie & Kelly," or sign up for our weekly newsletter.

PART ONE

HOW KNOWING YOUR PIXIETYPE CAN HELP SIMPLIFY YOUR LIFE

This part of the book is a crash course on personality/organizing type, understanding your PixieType, and what solutions will work best for you and those around you. While our organizing methods in future chapters refer to your "PixieType," the concept behind these categories go back millennia. Yes, you read that correctly: millennia. So sit back, relax, and enjoy the ride.

CHAPTER ONE

Why in the world should I care about personality when I just want to get organized?

Our work is based on our own thirty years of experience with personality-type theory, a concept that dates back to Plato and Hippocrates—yes, that's right; the ancient Greeks talked about these archetypes. (Some things never change.) But the real meat of our work is our ten years of proprietary research observing the home- and life-related organizational habits of our clients, friends, and family.

Understanding your personality type makes life easier. Let's say your idea of bliss is a cup of coffee and the newspaper by yourself, but you work as an equity trader, talking to people all day. After a workday, the best way for you to "recharge" would be to carve out at least thirty minutes of alone time. It doesn't mean you can't go out for drinks, laugh, and have fun with colleagues, but it's helpful to know that you'd be more relaxed if you'd gone for a walk by yourself or done some solo activity. And from there you can make it a priority—no apologies needed.

The same is true for organization. Knowing what you prefer to do with your shoes when you get home, where you dump your mail and how long it stays there, and when and how you make weekend plans will give you peace of mind like nothing else. At a minimum, you won't have to run around like a banshee *every* morning looking for your keys.

Why? Well, if you create a home for your keys where you tend to drop them by instinct as opposed to where everyone tells you they *should* reside, then you're more likely to find them the next morning. But it's bigger than keys: knowing that it's totally okay *not* to make your bed in the morning is a big revelation to some people. Let's say you detest having an unkempt bed. Well, you can stop apologizing for your "OCD" nature, because having it that way makes you feel relaxed, and there's nothing psychologically abnormal about that. Or let's say you have a filing cabinet you haven't touched in years because you pile paper like nobody's business, yet always think you should start filing away those piles. Guess what? You don't have to file. Seriously. We've got a different system, and it's pretty much what you already do, only with more structure around it. This is why knowing your personality type is so helpful: there's no need to feel bad about yourself, change all your habits, or reinvent the wheel to get and *stay* organized.

The distinguishing characteristic of our PixieType categorization is the research behind it—we studied people's organizational habits in their homes as professional organizers. We jokingly refer to ourselves as organizational anthropologists because we don't judge, but we do notice *everything*. That's likely the reason why so many friends of ours are always apologizing for their disorganization when we visit. . . . For the record, we do punch out and stop being Pixies in our free time.

It's also important to note that the PixieQuiz has not been exhaustively researched and psychometrically tested. It's just a quick and dirty way to figure out your organizing personality type. Who doesn't love a fun women's magazine–type quiz? We created easy-to-remember names—Classic, Fun, Organic, and Smart—for the four main PixieType categories (and, in our humble opinion, they're pretty catchy). We divide each of these four categories even further into two similar yet different personality types—thereby creating eight PixieTypes. We do this because within each of the four main PixieType groupings, there are still definitive dichotomies in how people make decisions, interact with the world around them, and structure their time. For example, Katie and our mother are both Organics, but Katie doesn't strive to structure her time (a trait of Organic Freedoms) whereas our mother (an Organic Structure) almost always strives to do so. Case in point: As we typed this sentence, Mom sent a text trying to confirm vacation dates for two months from now. Katie probably hasn't even thought about plans two weeks from now, let alone two months!

Some critics argue that personality-type theory is junk because people can get different results when they take the same personality assessment at different times. Well, of course they can if they answer differently—duh! Others complain that type theory unfairly pigeonholes people and doesn't account for personal growth. The truth is people change their answers on tests for a variety of reasons. Are you taking the assessment at home or at work? Does your response to a given situation vary depending on the people you're dealing with? Who are you comparing yourself with? You're never 100 percent one way or another, and recent memorable experiences can nudge you toward one response or another. In the end, you must identify with the personality description. Period. If it doesn't feel like you, it's not you.

Don't get us started on environmental influences. Two people with the same personality type are not clones. Everyone has different moms, dads, grandparents, siblings, teachers, friends, and life experiences. If you are a practical personality type with a dreamer mom you're probably less practical than someone like you who has a practical mom, and vice versa. Heck, even where you live leaves its mark. The same personality type born and raised in Madrid, land of late-night dinners and siestas, is going to have different habits than the same personality type raised in New York City, land of ten-hour workdays and lunch at your desk. The environmental influence is where you developed all of your *shoulds* about organizing. Our job is to help you pick and choose which of those *shoulds* to follow by revealing what works for your personality type and what doesn't. Our advice will help you better prioritize, so you're using your time more efficiently.

While helping clients handle home and life issues, we found five major and consistent differences in personality-type–related tendencies:

1. Certain personality types use To-Do lists religiously; others use them on occasion and never refer to them again.
2. Some types have a knack for décor . . . others, not so much.
3. Some types throw away cherished possessions with ease but collect plastic bags like grocery stores are going out of business; other types can't throw away sentimental things but have no problem ditching those plastic bags.
4. Some types make piles everywhere; others do it more sparingly.
5. Some types forget things hidden behind a door exist; others would be lost without their filing cabinet.

Many organizational tendencies correlate to personality type because they are hardwired, which is why we don't scold clients or expect them to make drastic changes to their predominant habits. Our solutions work around your reality.

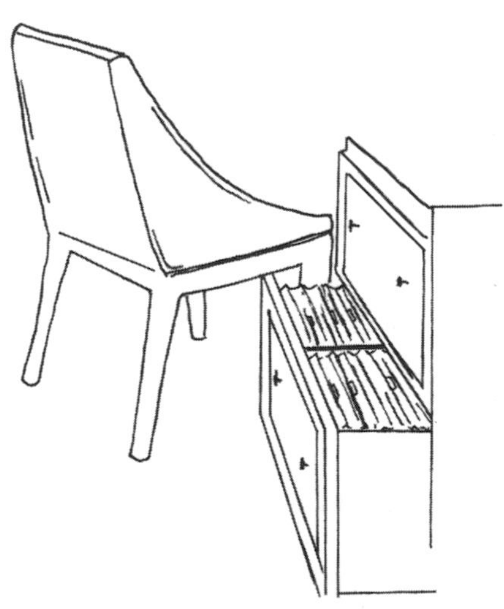

CHAPTER TWO

PixieType 101: Are you a Classic Pixie, a Fun Pixie, a Smart Pixie, or an Organic Pixie?

This chapter is the first step to figuring out who you are in our magical PixieType world. There are four overarching PixieTypes. We like to start with these because it's easier for people to choose between four, as opposed to eight. You might even recognize these four archetypes because, yes, they are almost stereotypical, but bear in mind: even though everyone is their own unique snowflake, real snowflakes all fall into eight basic snow categories (column crystals, plane crystals, combination column/plane crystals, aggregation of snow crystals, rimed snow crystals, germs of ice crystals, irregular snow particles, and other solid precipitation). . . . Okay, maybe not the best metaphor, but you get the gist. If you take our quiz and feel like the results aren't you—this might happen for a variety of reasons—then take a general gander at the next few pages, let your guard down, and see which of these four types sounds most like you. Who you are, how you organize, and what relaxes you are ultimately determined by the description with which you most identify. That's the real magic behind the PixieTypes.

THE CLASSIC PIXIE

TRADITIONAL, ORGANIZED

Classic Pixies tend to be the "guardians" of civilization, the world's worker bees, Little Red Hens doing all the work the rest of us take for granted. You are without question proverbial Type A's, often accused of or self-described as "OCD." Quite frankly, you are most likely responsible for the stereotype of the traditional, hardworking, loyal American. No, you're not always traditional, but you usually finish what you start, make dependable friends, and are rarely described as slackers. You feel best about life when striving toward a goal and getting things done. You love being organized and try to create routine and structure in your life.

You are known for being the cornerstones of society, for having a fundamental sense of right and wrong, for honoring traditions and customs. You guys are the ones who sign up, volunteer, and tend to say "yes" more than "no." You have a harder time relaxing and having fun, especially if you have something you planned to finish and haven't yet. You don't like to take risks unless you've firmly weighed all the pros and cons. And no, you are not lemmings, because you most certainly look very closely before you leap!

THE FUN PIXIE

ADVENTUROUS, PRACTICAL

Funs are well described as "artisans." You're the world's engineers and craftsmen, hands-on learners, people who are meticulous and tend to work in fine detail—on computers, in wood, clay, makeup, cuisine, etc.—without regard to how long it might take you because you want to get it done right. You enjoy getting lost in the moment so much that it means you're late, like, a lot. But we decided to call you "Fun" instead of "Artisan" because you're not all artists and you tend to be fun to hang out with because you're creative problem-solvers and occasional rule-breakers, yet you're also practical. Personality quizzes never seem to capture you: more than anything else, you hate being put in a box!

Focused on the *here* and *now*, Funs get things done but are flexible about the *when* and *how*. You are master improvisers.

THE ORGANIC PIXIE

IDEALISTIC, CREATIVE

Organics are those folks whose main goal in life is to help people, to thrust harmony upon the world like a 1960s freedom child. You are the idealists of the world, placing personal growth and relationships above all else. You feel best when you're helping make a difference—whether through work or your personal relationships.

For you, there's something crucial about changing the world by helping people reach their potential. This is more important to you than making bank or keeping up with the Joneses—that's just not your jam. Friendly cooperation is more like it. Our mom is an Organic and was an art therapist for years. When she retired, a patient's daughter sent her a thank-you letter for helping her mom get well. To her, this was tangible validation for her career, showing her that she had succeeded on her own personal journey by helping others achieve their best potential. You often feel alone in your battle to place authenticity and meaning ahead of achievement and ambition.

THE SMART PIXIE

INVENTIVE, CLEVER

Rationalists, or "Smarts," are the strategic thinkers of the world; the ones who tend to push themselves into positions of power without questioning why. Like Organics, you need to see your stuff; but unlike them, you don't care so much about how everyone is getting along. You guys can see how complex and interconnected the big picture actually is, and you know how to effect change within it to make it work better. As master delegators, you have no interest in the details, which are better left to other people to figure out. You are analytical and driven, and you set a high standard for everyone, including yourselves.

Smarts are the architects of change in this world. Somehow, you've always known this, and it's one of the reasons you stand out. You're the ones who always end up running things, even if you consciously try not to do it. So many CEOs, presidents, and other leaders are Smarts. It's probably because you're intellectually curious and adept complex problem-solvers—and maybe even a little bit smarter than the next fellow.

Okay, that's the main four. Anything seem familiar? If you're not entirely comfortable restricting yourself to just one of the "big four," we are not surprised. Sometimes you need to dig deeper. There are nuances you might recognize better if you take the quiz in the next chapter and read about the eight PixieTypes in Chapter 4 (page 26). But remember: no one is ever going to identify 100 percent with any category because, as we said earlier, there are tons of environmental influences that shape you. What we're talking about is your innate, natural tendencies—habits you fall back on when nobody is looking. These tendencies are the personality equivalent of whether you favor your left hand or your right. Do you prefer making weekend plans in advance, or seeing where the weekend will take you? Do you prefer working with innovative "out there" ideas, or commonsense, implementable ideas? It's never one way or the other in every scenario, but everyone has tendencies. Read ahead and take the quiz, which will help shed light on which PixieType you actually are.

CHAPTER THREE

Who the heck are you? Take the PixieQuiz!

On the next few pages is our PixieQuiz with directions on how to tabulate it. You can also take it online at http://www.pixiesdidit.com/get-started/pixies-personality-quiz/, where computer code tabulates it for you. When taking either one, don't be tempted to answer questions in a way that makes you look super-organized or laid back or whatever it is you, ahem, think you *should* be. If you do it that way, the result won't be *you*, and our solutions won't be as helpful. Yes, we all know being on time is valued in our society, but if you easily lose track of time, own up to it. Lots of people will admit the same to themselves if they're being honest—there's no shame or blame here. There are no wrong answers.

After you get your quiz result—and this is *muy importante*—check out the different personality types in Chapter 4 (page 26), and make sure you identify with the result. Also, do the ultimate "BS Barometer" by having a close friend read your personality result and tell you whether it sounds like you. We've found that these are often the best ways to tell if your responses are accurate. For example, if you're often ten minutes late but don't realize it, your best friend will call you out on it.

1. **You're into this new hit crime show that features two equally compelling and smoking-hot FBI agents. Who do you identify with most? (C'mon, be honest with yourself.)**
   a. The investigator who goes by hunches and gut instinct, like Fox Mulder.
   b. The detective who relies on facts and clues, like Dana Scully.

2. **You're sitting in a middle seat in coach on an airplane. The people on either side blather on and on. Who do you hope falls asleep first? (And yes, personally, we want them both to fall asleep. But if you had one Ambien®, whose drink do you spike?)**
   a. The imaginative person full of novel ideas.
   b. The practical person with a lot of commonsense ideas.

3. **Choose the statement below that best fits you.**
   a. I like to get the big picture and then drill into the facts.
   b. I like to drill into the facts and then get the big picture.

4. **Your best friend has to choose the label below that sounds most like you. Which one would he/she pick?**
   a. Dreamer.
   b. Doer.

5. **This is a "Deep Thought" type question (does anyone else remember Jack Handey?). If your conscience could speak, what would it say?**
   a. Dream bigger.
   b. The devil is in the details.

6. **You find yourself in Indonesia with a wrinkly, old medicine man. (Yes, we stole this from *Eat Pray Love*, the movie. Feel free to imagine yourself as Julia Roberts or Javier Bardem in this scenario.) Which of the following wise sayings does he offer after studying your palm?**
   a. You are most often drawn toward ingenuity.
   b. You are most often drawn toward realism.

7. **You're an equity investor—someone who has a lot of money to burn but only invests in companies likely to generate a lot of money. Which company do you invest in?**
   a. The company with the bold, untested idea that might change the world and deliver one massive payday.
   b. The company with the tried-and-true idea that might deliver a steady stream of cash.

8. **In a glorified movie adaption of your life, which character would you play?**
   a. I'd be the character that implements a brilliant last-minute plan to save the day (e.g., MacGyver).
   b. I'd be the character that implements a brilliant plan ahead of time (e.g., Sherlock Holmes).

9. **Which one of these statements captures your general approach toward life?**
   a. I often think I should structure my life, but more often than not, I tend to just see what happens and enjoy the ride.
   b. While I often wish I could relax and enjoy the ride, I'm just not comfortable unless I have created a structure to make something happen.

10. **Pick the statement that best fits you.**
   a. Spontaneous fun rocks!
   b. Spontaneous fun rocks when there's time and the chores are finished!

11. **Pick the statement that best fits you.**
   a. I'm less aware of time and tend to run late.
   b. I tend to pay attention to time and am usually prompt.

12. **Pick the statement that best fits you. (Yeah, another statement pair question—you got a problem with that?)**
   a. I like to keep my options open.
   b. I like to settle things quickly.

13. **Social weekend plans . . . What's your usual strategy?**
   a. See what comes up when the weekend rolls around.
   b. Make plans in advance.

14. **Left to your own devices—that is, not the unsolicited advice of every organizer, boss, teacher, etc.—you:**
   a. Write To-Do lists, sometimes, but more often than not you don't need them to get things done—it's in your head.
   b. Write out daily To-Do lists or use a master schedule and enjoy crossing off items.

15. **As a whopping generality, when push comes to shove, usually, more often than not, etc., when people ask how it's going, you tend to . . .**
   a. Be open with your emotions.
   b. Keep emotions close to your vest.

16. **Imagine you're in some strange alternate universe where everyone has a personal crest and motto. Which motto would you choose?**
   a. Peace and Harmony
   b. Logic is Harmony

17. **In your experience, what's the best tactic for getting your way?**
   a. Gentle persuasion.
   b. Assertiveness.

18. **The sky is the limit—you can work in any field you want! Which is more appealing to you?**
   a. A career where people and communication are most important.
   b. A career where logic and precision are paramount.

19. **Pick the statement that best fits you.**
   a. I tend to make decisions with my heart and strive to be compassionate.
   b. I tend to make decisions with my head and strive to be fair.

20. **We all have flaws. Which of the following do you think most people you know would choose to describe you?**
   a. Sometimes I'm too idealistic, agreeable, or indirect.
   b. Sometimes I'm too task-oriented, aloof, or brutally honest.

21. **When you are working with a group on a problem, what tends to be your main objective?**
   a. Reaching a "win/win" solution that everyone can agree on.
   b. Reaching a solution supported by facts, regardless of who "wins" and who "loses."

Tally your results!

Put an "X" or a "✓" in the column for your answer for each question, and then tally how many you have in Column A vs. Column B. Directions for tabulating it all are on the next page.

Piling			Scheduling			Decluttering		
Question	A	B	Question	A	B	Question	A	B
1			8			15		
2			9			16		
3			10			17		
4			11			18		
5			12			19		
6			13			20		
7			14			21		
Tally			Tally			Tally		

Piling

If you got 4 or more **A**'s, you're an **Organic** or a **Smart**. Now go tally the "Scheduling" section.

If you got 4 or more **B**'s, you're a **Fun** or a **Classic**. Now go tally the "Scheduling" section.

Scheduling

ORGANICS/SMARTS: If you got four or more **A**'s, you're either an **Organic** or **Smart Freedom**. If you got four or more **B**'s, then you're either an **Organic** or **Smart Structure**. Now go tally the "Decluttering" section.

FUNS/CLASSICS: If you got four or more **A**'s, then you're a **Fun**. If you got four or more **B**'s, then you're a **Classic**. Now go tally the "Decluttering" section.

Decluttering

ORGANIC/SMART FREEDOMS: If you got four or more **A**'s, then you're an **Organic Freedom**. If you got four or more **B**'s, then you're a **Smart Freedom**.

ORGANIC/SMART STRUCTURES: If you got four or more **A**'s, then you're an **Organic Structure**. If you got four or more **B**'s, then you're a **Smart Structure**.

FUNS: If you got four or more **A**'s, then you're a **Fun Freedom**. If you got four or more **B**'s, then you're a **Fun Structure**.

CLASSICS: If you got four or more **A**'s, then you're a **Classic Freedom**. If you got four or more **B**'s, then you're a **Classic Structure**.

CHAPTER FOUR

How the eight PixieTypes organize home and life

There are eight PixieTypes because we divide each of the four overarching PixieTypes—Classic, Fun, Organic, and Smart—into two similar yet different types. Having eight types allows us to get closer to capturing you and to more accurately demonstrate how each PixieType prefers to structure their homes and lives. After you've identified your true PixieType, scan through the other types described in this chapter to see if you can identify other people in your lives. Doing so will give you more understanding of who you are *not*, and why different people annoy the crap out of you sometimes. For instance, just because a Classic relies on her daily To-Do list to get things done doesn't mean her Fun husband can't keep track without one; it's simply in his head. His forgetting to do something every once in a while isn't a sign that he needs to adopt a written To-Do list; it's a sign he's human. Even Classics forget to do things on their beloved To-Do list—or "My Precious," as Classic Kelly calls hers—on occasion.

CLASSICS

A place for everything and everything in its place

It's not surprising that when people picture the age-old stereotypical fanny-pack–wearing American tourist, they're usually picturing Classics. Even if most of you had the good sense to ditch your fanny pack in the '90s, you represent most Americans and likely wrote half the organizational rules out there. Heck, you probably invented the filing cabinet. You run a tight ship and are usually the most competent to "properly" run a household (the quotation marks indicate that this is technically subjective). As a Classic, you're either a Classic Structure, who uses logic to make decisions, or a Classic Freedom, who uses more subjective criteria.

Classic Structure

A modern-day June Cleaver's not-always-warm-and-fuzzy twin

1. Invented traditional organizing
2. Likes things hidden, orderly, and decluttered
3. Tends to be detail-oriented and into scheduling
4. Does well with routine
5. Makes advance plans
6. Files more than others
7. Piles "politely"
8. Prefers physical To-Do lists

Classic Structures essentially make the gears of society work, come hell or high water. You prefer to plan and structure your days and jive with routine. Order gives you peace of mind. You are punctual, tidy, friendly, logical decision-makers. The latter gives you a bit of an edge, and we don't mean this in a bad way. You believe in fairness but tend to put logic ahead of people when solving problems.

There is purpose behind almost all of your housekeeping routines or rules. For example, a majority of you make your bed in the morning because it makes the bed feel clean at bedtime. However, we met a Classic Structure who instead pulled the bed sheets all the way back in the morning to air them out during the day for much the same purpose—a different solution, for sure, but there is logic and purpose there. And this is why you guys make up the largest percentage of home jerry-riggers. This facile use of logic means you're decisive and have the easiest time throwing clutter out. Details are also one of your fortes, which is why the minutiae of running a household and filing papers away can seem easy for you.

As for where you can get tripped up? You often cram things in a space because it's the proper home, even though you've run out of space, and you accumulate clutter when you're too busy to put decluttering on your To-Do list. You often have a hard time delegating tasks that you're capable of doing but *shouldn't*. Finally, some of your organizational solutions can be too utilitarian, aka "ugly"—especially if you are male.

Classic Freedom

Um, a modern-day June Cleaver

1. Invented traditional organizing
2. Likes things hidden and orderly
3. Tends to be detail-oriented and into scheduling
4. Does well with routine
5. Makes advance plans
6. Files more than others
7. Piles "politely"
8. Prefers physical To-Do lists

Classic Freedoms are quintessential homemakers—we mean this as a compliment—and this is true whether you're a housewife, a working mom, single, or a guy. You're tidy, you're punctual, you're warm, and you're efficient. You plan out your days using calendars and To-Do lists, and you only get tripped up when the routine changes. As the underpinnings of society and often the grease that gets those gears humming, you make running a household look like a walk in the park. This is because you are detail-oriented, which is also why you easily find things that are hidden away.

Unlike Classic Structures, Classic Freedoms are value-based, subjective decision-makers. You base decisions on past experience and how things will impact people more often than you use logic. For example, you don't like your husband's baseball caps hanging on his bedroom mirror because . . . well . . . you simply don't like it. You're right vis-à-vis the ball caps (it looks terrible), but this is technically a subjective judgment, not logic.

Don't get us wrong: there is a lot of logic to your organization. You file with the best of them, you are highly practical, and you are thrifty when need be. Your organizational "waterloos," if anything, are saying "yes" to too many requests, forgetting to do things that are not on your To-Do list, not properly prioritizing, and trying to do it all in one day. It's not easy for you to think outside of the box for organizational solutions, and you have a harder time clearing clutter than more-decisive types. For instance, you swiftly throw out all of your cheap glass vases once you have nice ones, but you can't part with an ugly, unused, glass jar vase you made at summer camp.

FUNS

You want me to commit to a weekend away twelve months from now?!?

When a couple hires us and one of them justifies it by saying "I'm not one specific personality type; I am a little bit of them all," or "I don't believe in that crap," we know exactly who you are: a Fun. Yes, you are easygoing, sometimes adventurous, and adept at living in the moment. However, you are also firmly grounded in reality and the practical details of life and work, which means the bills get paid and work gets done even if you misplace things or rarely have a written To-Do list. You guys are somewhat of an organizing enigma: messy in some areas and super-tidy down to the smallest detail in other areas. The parts of your house that are best organized are related to the areas of life in which you have a passion—that is, your closet if you're a clotheshorse, or the kitchen if you love to cook. Funs, like Classics, are separated into two different types based on whether they use logic (Fun Structures) or subjective criteria (Fun Freedoms) to make decisions.

Fun Structure

Bond . . . James Bond

1. Tends to be orderly and detail-oriented (when it matters to you)
2. Prefers flexible scheduling
3. Does best accomplishing things in the moment
4. Relies on habit more than routine
5. Files when given an easy system but can default to piling
6. Prefers mental To-Do lists
7. Excels at decluttering

We gave Fun Structures a cool title, but don't get ahead of yourself, because some of you could also be better described as "Computer Programmer" or "MacGyver." You are logical, detail-oriented decision-makers who believe in fairness and tend to put logic before people when solving problems. But that's why you're amazing in a crisis. You're also easygoing and spontaneous—umm, you have to be if you're a spy, right?—yet still practical through it all, keeping your possessions neater than most. Your in-the-moment decisiveness comes in handy for an international man (or woman) of mystery who needs to make lifesaving judgment calls in the nick of time or, say, throw away clutter before it gets unruly. The clutter you do accumulate tends to be pragmatic in nature—there is a logical reason you kept it—but you also have collections that reflect your passions.

Fun Structures can find their own organizational path, but you can file with the best of them if someone sets up a logical filing system for you. Even though written To-Do lists are a no-go, using electronic devices to set up automated reminders is a great tool for remembering To Dos and events. Your organizational kryptonite is consistently being late, especially for social gatherings. You tend to put things off, don't like making a ton of firm advance plans, and are loath to create organizational systems for rooms and areas you don't care about. You also hate doing insanely boring maintenance projects like cleaning out a closet when you're not in the mood. When you can figure out how to make these events and tasks more *fun—or perhaps more dangerous, Mr. Bond*—nothing will stop your organizational dominance.

Fun Freedom

Timmy Bond, James's cousin

1. Tends to be orderly and detail-oriented (when it matters to you)
2. Prefers flexible scheduling
3. Does best accomplishing things in the moment
4. Is okay with routine but likes to mix it up
5. Files when given an easy system but can default to piling
6. Prefers mental To-Do lists

Fun Freedoms are also spontaneous like a spy and a massive help in a crisis—you always seem to land on your feet. You're easygoing and know how to enjoy life (*carpe diem!*), but you don't ignore practical matters like organization. Well, sometimes you do. You base decisions on past experience and also consider how things might impact other people. Sometimes you're logical, sometimes you're not. You do your best organizational work when you're inspired to do it, and when you're busy or doing much more interesting things—which is a long list—the mess can get a little out of hand.

Fun Freedoms do well with most traditional physical organizing systems—filing cabinets, like with like, etc.—and you often only find yourself disorganized or overwhelmed with clutter because you haven't had the time or inclination to focus on it. You tend to have collections of things that reflect your loves or passions, and you are often the best at maintaining color-coded organization. Your organizational stumbling blocks include poor scheduling, your dislike of boring routines, failure to get rid of extraneous clutter, and postponing of tasks (aka procrastinating). Find a fun way to do these things with your cousin James, and we suspect you'll start to think you're invincible.

ORGANICS

Please don't touch my piles—thanks so much

You are almost always kind, and you let (dis)order develop *organically*, as the name implies. You tend to get more overwhelmed by physical stuff in your life because, even if you know where things are, it doesn't always *look* like it. You have the hardest time letting go of your stuff out of all the PixieTypes. It's either because you feel guilty, or because it seems a waste. Result? Decision postponed, stuff accumulated. You also tend to surround yourself with sentimental tchotchkes, photographs, books, and things that remind you of the good times in your life, and there's often a story behind each object. The Organic Structures among you prefer structure and are masters of the Day Planner and written To-Do lists, while the Organic Freedoms tend to take life as it comes and are always trying to keep a written To-Do list, to no avail.

Organic Structure

A landscaped English garden

1. Likes things out in the open vs. hidden
2. Has a more visual memory
3. Is not always detail-oriented
4. Prefers fixed scheduling and advance plans
5. Tends to pile things
6. Prefers physical To-Do lists
7. Does well with routine

Organic Structures can appreciate the seemingly wild beauty that is a proper English garden, but you also know that most require quite a bit of planning and forethought. They're also inherently practical because they don't require much maintenance, like you and your home. You prefer to live life in a scheduled, structured environment, meaning you like a tidy house and use a Day Planner of some sort. It may not be perfect, but it's good enough.

Your piles are not the result of postponed decision-making, but rather a way to keep things out so you can remember them, and it's incredibly irritating if someone files them away for you (their term for it is *tidying*; yours is the opposite). Sure, you have a To-Do list and a planner, but sometimes things don't make it into those. Having things out in the open serves as a visual reminder, and if you already switched to a digital calendar, you probably miss the physical act of writing things out and seeing them (we have some Organic Structure clients who use a digital calendar but put key events on an analog wall calendar). You like routines and generally stick to them, but you are not rigid, as you always see the big picture and instinctively prioritize quite well.

Organic Structure organizational stumbling blocks are haphazard piles, refusing to let go of sentimental *and* practical items, ignoring important details, forgetting about things that are hidden away, and overthinking an organizational dilemma. Remember: once you get in over your head, organizationally speaking—i.e., a massive amount of clutter in an attic or basement—it's too much for you to do on your own. Get a friend to help, or hire someone.

Organic Freedom

The wild beauty of the English moors

1. Likes things out in the open vs. hidden
2. Needs to see things to remember them
3. Prefers flexible scheduling, but recurring appointments are easier to remember
4. Detests boring routine, but an ingrained or fun routine can be used to accomplish much
5. Does best finishing things in the moment
6. Piles things, almost egregiously so
7. Prefers mental To-Do lists, unless overwhelmed

As an Organic Freedom, you certainly appreciate the grandiose beauty of an English garden (and the low-maintenance upkeep, since you're not crazy about frequent routines like weeding and trimming). If you have one yourself, it most likely came together after you randomly chose a bunch of perennials you liked. You are dreamers who prefer to experience life rather than control it. Planning and logistics are not really your bag, but you're not out to lunch, either. Even without tons of structured plans, it all eventually turns up roses, or at least some variation of wild heather on an English moor.

Organic Freedoms don't mind routine but easily break it, especially when feeling stifled (even subconsciously). Day Planners are often a waste of money, even though you're always trying some new system to get more organized. Piles are rarely planned; they just happen—usually as the symptom of postponed decision-making ("Where should I put this? . . . Umm . . . I'll put it there for now"). To-Do lists are pretty well organized in your head, but occasional written ones are handy if you're overwhelmed. Electronic reminders and sending yourself e-mails to do things are preferable to an actual To-Do list, which is easily misplaced (at least the pencil-and-paper version). You have a visual memory, so seeing is remembering, which is another reason why you leave things out or in piles.

Whatever you can get done in the moment gets done; anything put off until tomorrow could get done tomorrow or four months from now or never, because you waited too long. Your organizational pitfalls sometimes *feel* as if they encompass everything in this buttoned-up world, but really they are only accumulating clutter, being on time, forgetting about items hidden away, putting things back in their homes, procrastinating, and overanalyzing organizational solutions.

SMARTS

Under no circumstances are you to touch my piles. Are we clear?

Remember that game Mastermind®? It's the classic two-person board game of logic and deduction where you try to break your opponent's code in ten moves or less. That's what we think of when we think of you. How does that translate into how you organize your home and life? Well, you have your distinct opinions about how a home should look, but you'd much rather have someone else execute it. As the leaders of the world, you long ago mastered the art of delegation. Unless you *love* cleaning and tidying and organizing details, you'll leave that to others . . . with your guidance, of course. While Smart Structures prefer structure and planning, living and dying by their Day Planners and strategically orchestrated To-Do lists, Smart Freedoms find it difficult to use a calendar, preferring to keep things in their head, where the possibilities are limitless.

Smart Structure

The President

1. Likes things out in the open vs. hidden
2. Has a more visual memory
3. Isn't always detail-oriented
4. Prefers fixed scheduling and advance plans
5. Tends to pile things
6. Prefers physical To-Do lists

Smart Structure has personality traits that the majority of Americans probably imagine a president or great general would have: bold yet practical, decisive yet pensive. You prefer to live life in a scheduled and structured way. Your big-picture thinking skills means you use Day Planners—or their electronic equivalent—with aplomb. You also enjoy routine (tennis is on Wednesdays,

Fridays you prefer to keep plans to a minimum, etc.) and a tidy, well-appointed house. Incompetence in others is hard to bear, and you surround yourself with talented people to whom you can delegate things that are not your core competencies whenever possible. Household maintenance is done by a cleaning lady or your spouse. Sometimes you come off as a bit gruff, even though you don't mean to be.

The details of maintaining a household can seem a bit tedious, but when it's important to you, you do it and you do it *right*. You usually finish what you start. Even with a secretary or personal assistant and reams of filing cabinets, you tend to surround yourself with paper piles, but there's always a structure to them—and you detest it when someone disturbs them. You need to see things to easily remember them, and you often have a lot of items that represent some part of your life's work or accomplishments, be they awards, photos, books, or other objects. Parting with them doesn't often cross your mind.

Your organizational challenges include being inflexible with your schedule, overlooking seemingly innocuous details, holding on to what you deem important clutter, forgetting about things that are hidden away, and digging your heels in when someone else's advice is different from what you think is best.

Smart Freedom

Don Draper

1. Likes things out in the open vs. hidden
2. Needs to see things to remember them
3. Prefers flexible scheduling, but recurring appointments are easier to remember
4. Detests boring routine, but an ingrained or fun routine can be used to accomplish much
5. Does best finishing things in the moment
6. Piles things, almost egregiously so
7. Prefers mental To-Do lists, unless overwhelmed

Smart Freedoms prefer to understand and experience life instead of controlling and structuring it. You don't live your life by routines (tennis is on Wednesdays unless you don't feel like it, Friday is for what you want to do or what comes up, etc.), and you most certainly don't use Day Planners or written To-Do lists. You're someone who will jot down ideas, but the big-picture planning is in your head for the most part. You often have a vision for your home, and it looks amazing when you're done. Even though you can be pragmatic, your grand visions often overpower those sensibilities. You need to see things to know where they are, so you tend to have piles of stuff around (and they're not precisely purposeful, with any rhyme or reason).

Smart Freedoms tend to have random things hidden away in drawers or cabinets because tiny details are not your strong suit. Often, random clutter and disorganization are the result of postponed decision-making about where to put something that doesn't have an obvious home, or simply the result of mental preoccupation while you're putting things away. Organizational challenges include being overwhelmed at implementing your visions for your house, overlooking the minutiae of managing your life, not planning ahead or finishing things, holding on to items you don't think of as clutter, and procrastinating. But before we leave you thinking "Wait, what *am* I good at?," remember: like Don Draper in *Mad Men*, you tend to come up with brilliant and creative ideas, seemingly out of nowhere, and you're a logical dreamer.

* * * * * * * * * * * * * * * * * * *

Do you see yourself in any of these descriptions? Keep in mind that our life stories are all different, shaping us into the unique and amazing individuals that we are. So either pick the one (or two, or even three) that sound *most* like you—or just use the organizational solutions that make the most sense.

Now it's time to get and *stay* organized—the easy way.

PART TWO

THE MAGIC PIXIE PRESCRIPTION, OR "PIXIEDUST," IF YOU WILL

We go through each room in your home in the order that clutter and disorganization generally start and flourish. Each part of your house is dependent upon each other, but it all comes in through the main door, so that's where we begin. Each chapter has universal solutions that will work for almost everybody, and then we get into the magical "PixieDust" sections offering unique solutions that work best for your individual PixieType. Together, they will bring you closer to the magical reality of an organized home—that stays organized.

CHAPTER FIVE

The Entryway

The main entryway to your home: it's not only the first introduction the world has to your little patch; it's also how the world's detritus—junk mail, sports gear, luggage, etc.—gets into your home. This means there needs to be an organizational system already set up to handle this stuff, or the old "default" system will take over (i.e., the dread pirate of organization: *clutter*). Now, by "entryway" we mean both where you walk in the door, as well as the first available, sensible spot to put things down. "Available" and "sensible" are often two separate spots if there's not enough room for everything right by the door and/or you want your literal entryway to be clutter-free. Regardless, it's the first stop on the clutter train, and—here more than anywhere else—you need to be true to your personality type because you use it most when you're rushing out the door or exhausted on the way in and therefore less able to flex your nondominant sides. However, a few compromises are inevitable, especially when living with others.

UNIVERSAL SOLUTIONS

Entryway Essentials for *All Types*

- Purge!
- Purchase matching, sturdy coat hangers.
- Install hooks.
- Give your keys a home.
- MEASURE . . . TWICE.
- Buy a bunch of bins.
- Avoid cheap shoe racks.
- Store kids' stuff at their height.
- Buy entryway rugs.
- Get an umbrella stand.
- Create a system for incoming paper.
- Have a wastebasket nearby.
- Label every bin (unless you live alone and aren't a Classic).
- Communicate your new system.

Purge!

One reason people don't hang up coats—throwing them over chairs instead—is that there are too many coats and sundries already *in* the coat closet. Call it what you will—decluttering, pruning, or purging—but nine times out of ten, everyone needs to do it. Get rid of unused coats, totes, and accessories, and relocate anything in there that you don't use or wear on a seasonal basis. Our rule of thumb is: unworn items for two seasons are goners. Bag the items you can part with—doing so inhibits many from retrieving items and makes it easier to transport stuff out—and then donate or sell them in the most expedient, ethical way possible. Just remember to advise other household members of your purge before doing so.

Before some of you panic and dismiss us as your garden-variety clutter fascists, we make allowances for what to keep and how to go about ditching stuff, based on each PixieType, before chapter's end. As for tote bags, you

> **PixieTip!**
>
> Let other people in the house know you are purging, and make sure they're okay with your choices. Sometimes it's better to bag things first, wait a bit, and then tell people. If they don't miss anything, chances are they won't even bother to go through the bag.
>
> Living in big cities with overpriced real estate makes organizing a pain because you need to shove a lot of things into one closet. The trick is to ensure that you have structured homes for everything; otherwise, it'll be a mosh pit.

don't need more than three or four. You don't. Really. Try to limit yourself to the five best—ditto for fancy paper retail shopping bags—and donate the rest. Outerwear accessories multiply faster than bunnies. Follow the same two-season rule. Mismatched gloves should get the heave-ho at season's end. They're not socks—you'll never find the other one, as it probably fell out of your pocket. While you're at it, go ahead and ditch the mismatched socks, too. Most of them are never coming back. You can't imagine how free you'll feel, like Julie Andrews on top of the Austrian Alps.

After decluttering, if your coat closet is still packed, ensure that everything in it needs to be in that location. Often this closet can become a bit of a "junk" closet because, in the heat of a cleanup moment, most of us are guilty of stashing random stuff in here just to get it out of the hallway or living room. Get rid of anything that doesn't make sense, or that's technically not needed in an entryway closet—sports equipment, cleaning supplies, board games, old photos, outdoor holiday lights . . . (yes, we've seen it all!). Pare down the themes in there as much as possible.

Purchase matching, sturdy coat hangers

No arguments. That's right: *No. More. Wire. Hangers!* This is a minimal expense with never-ending dividends of how much easier your life will become, never searching for a coat or struggling to stuff one in the closet, not to mention the aesthetic pleasure of a row of coats lined up neatly. Count how many coats you have, and then buy at least five more hangers than that for guest coats and new ones.

Install hooks

These are miracle workers. Essential for all types, they get things off the floor fast and easy, and they also make use of vertical space, which is always more plentiful than horizontal. Hooks do double duty as "keeping the peace" diplomats. Have trouble getting your mate to hang up her coat on a hanger? Give her a hook. Have lots of bags on the closet floor? Put up hooks and get those bags off the floor. Yes, some types will "abuse" these hooks and pile too much stuff on them, but it's still better than having jackets and coats draped all over your furniture.

Besides your traditional coat rack, you need hooks mounted inside your closet—solidly, by a handyman who knows his stuff—and two to four hooks at varying heights on the back of a solid closet door, depending on the closet depth (make sure you can still close the door). Just two hooks wherever there is room adds instant organization, whether you live alone or in a larger household, and the more the merrier.

PixieTip!

Coat racks are not substitutes for closets, unless you literally own only four or five coats. If you have to lift two coats off a hook to get one out, you're abusing the coat rack. What has it ever done to you?

Keep an entryway jar or bowl for coins, so they're in one place and you don't have loose change everywhere or weighing your purse down. Pick a jar large enough to handle a month's worth of coins, something attractive but not irreplaceable (e.g., a Ming vase is a dumb idea).

Give your keys a home

Store keys where you dump everything when you arrive home. Keys either go in a designated bowl or on a teacup hook. However, some people find it easiest to put keys right back in their purse or jacket pocket (hey, if it ain't broke, don't fix it). Whatever you do, put them in the same place. If the latter is impossible, consider a keyless door lock.

Measure . . . twice

Once you've cleared things out of the entryway to the best of your ability, you need to get bins (primarily for outerwear accessories). But before you do so—before you buy *anything* for this room or, frankly, anywhere—measure the closet and the space where these items will rest, and have these measurements at hand when you shop. Even measure under-door clearances for entryway rugs or doormats. If you are a human, we recommend measuring twice because humans frequently mess up basic things like measuring, which is super-annoying when you have to return something but forget and find it in the back of a closet ten years later.

Buy a bunch of bins

You need at least half an inch (13 mm) on either side for baskets and bins to pull out easily on a closet shelf. Remember, bins will look awful if they hang over the edge of a shelf or table, so make sure they fit. What kind and how many bins you need depends on *who* you are, so read about your PixieType later on in this chapter to find out. Everyone needs bins for outerwear accessories, as there is no other way to corral everything. (Plus, bins get as close as possible to cubbyholes, which are beloved by most everybody who went to kindergarten.) If you have the room, get individual cubbyholes (they fit nicely in tiny places), and label them, too. Naturally, some caveats exist by PixieType. If you can't go this route, a coat rack with a bench underneath is a good substitute. We're not fans of hanging-sweater bins in bedrooms, but they work wonders in the front-hall closet. Better yet: their shoe equivalent is smaller and great for stuffing hats and gloves—and perfect for kids!

Another place to put bins is the back of a door. The Container Store® offers a door and wall rack system with narrow wire baskets mounted on one track. We think of it as PixieMagic!

Label every bin (unless you live alone and aren't a Classic)

Labels in entryways aren't technically necessary, but they're helpful in a multiple-person household where people need to locate items that have been sorted when they're not around. Also, life can be very hectic, and even the best of us can forget where things are. Labels can also keep you from getting lazy and stuffing things you don't know what to do with in an empty corner somewhere. (Yes, all types are guilty of this at times.)

Avoid cheap shoe racks

We've got personality-specific shoe solutions in each section, but as a general rule, cheap, multilayer (more than two) shoe racks don't work in front-hall closets, because long coats hang down and impede seeing or retrieving shoes, regardless of who you are. Communal shoe bins are great if you have young kids, but they are not a universal solution (we've seen Smarts and Classics who refuse to treat their shoes so poorly). Weed out excess shoes as you did with coats, totes, and accessories. The two-season rule also applies here, but notify others before ditching them.

Store kids' stuff at their height

This seems like common sense, but you'd be surprised. . . . Put kids' things where they can reach them, especially if you don't want them throwing their coats and gloves on the floor. Bins for outerwear accessories should have easy access on the floor, and coat racks should be mounted at their height. Add some hooks low on a wall or in a closet if necessary. Label everything. Outgrown kids' clothes go immediately into storage or out the door.

Buy entryway rugs

It almost goes without saying, but there needs to be a rug in the entryway. Some of you think it'll only get dirty and then you'll have to clean it, but that's the point. The rug is supposed to soak up dirt up front, so it's not tracked everywhere in the home. If it's an informal entryway, get something practical and inexpensive, like a sisal rug or an indoor/outdoor rug. Get two so you can switch them while one is

PixieTip!

Doormats prevent people from doing crazy things like one Classic Structure we know and love who, when it's raining, puts *newspapers* down to soak up water and dirt at his threshold. Um, newspapers are for reading, recycling, or papier-mâché.

being cleaned—Classics, get ones you can toss in the washer so you're not constantly spot-cleaning. Believe it or not, many PixieTypes would never clean the entryway rug unless some drunken guest spilled red wine on it. Even then, there are a few PixieTypes who would take three or more months to attend to that accident in a meaningful way. If it is a formal entryway, get a nice rug, but also have a doormat where you can really brush off the dirt, grime, and water from your shoes.

> **PixieTip!**
>
> If a Winnebago® has a bigger closet than yours, a space-saving idea is to use a hook or two to store umbrellas on the door or inside wall of the closet.
>
> It will be a while before everybody reads news and magazines on their iPad®s, so until this day comes, keep official homes for incoming newspapers and magazines nearby. This way you can separate them from more pressing items like bills and invites.

Get an umbrella stand

These days you may need two umbrella stands: a traditional tall, upright stand for big, traditional umbrellas, and a small bin for compact ones. The former can live in or out of a closet, depending on its size, its beauty, whether there is space in the closet, and whether you can stand the visible clutter of umbrellas. If you can't, then get umbrellas you like and give away garish ones. Yes, we're serious: it's an absurd touch that will make you happy, and life is too short not to be.

Create a system for incoming paper

No matter who you are, you need to have a system set up to handle paper coming into your house. What this system should look like varies *widely* by PixieType. It starts with a household inbox on the closest designated entryway surface—console table or countertop—where you tend to dump things as you enter. Note that a dining-room or kitchen table is a horrible surface on which to locate the main tray, even temporarily. The inbox is ideally an open box or tray that can hold legal-size documents and packages, but there are caveats for each PixieType. You can have just one, or give each person in the house his or her own.

Have a wastebasket nearby

You need a recycling bin or wastebasket wherever you dump and/or go through your mail, although there is some variability in this directive depending on your PixieType.

Communicate your new system

You might think your new entryway system is self-explanatory, but it is not. Walk anyone regularly working or living in your home through your system, explaining where everything goes and *why.* When people don't know the *why* behind a system, they respect it less, even if you've labeled things like a madman.

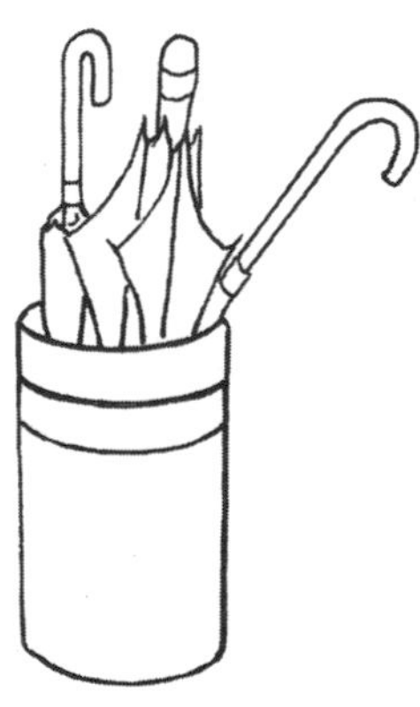

Entryway

1 Entryway closets are often the default location for the vacuum cleaner, but they are not the best place to store one.

2 A collection of mismatched hangers with coats that are too heavy and falling off.

3 The front-hall closet is not an appropriate home for a sleeping bag!

4 Inappropriate storage alert: Did you remember there are board games in here?

5 There's no place to store and retrieve scarves, gloves, and hats.

6 Can you find the umbrella in here?

7 Behold: the boot mosh pit. Like the broken-window theory, this mess begets more mess.

8 Newspapers and magazines don't have a home, so they end up on the floor.

9 Where's that wedding invitation again? The entryway table is too small to handle the paper influx.

1 Use an entryway tray to stash incoming mail. Funs, Organic Freedoms, and Smart Freedoms: beware it doesn't get too full.

2 Designate this spot as a proper home for umbrellas or a bin to stash trash as you sort mail. This is essential for Organics and Smarts.

3 Coat racks and hooks are essential for Organic Freedoms and Smart Freedoms.

4 Labels make it easy to remember where things are and where to put them.

5 Bins organize accessories. Transparent bins are essential for Organics and Smarts.

6 Install as many hooks as your closet can hold for scarves, jackets, and bags.

7 Matching, sturdy wooden hangers make it easier to see what's hanging and properly hold heavy coats.

8 Coat hooks are essential for kids, and these are positioned at their height.

9 Shoe bins hold boots in place. Give everyone in the household their own bin. Bins are essential for Organics and Smarts, though shelves are preferable for Funs and Classics.

10 Hanging shoe cubbies are a great solution to stash everyday hats and gloves.

11 Matching bins give a home to newspapers and magazines and can also double as recycling containers.

12 Use an easy one-step bowl solution to drop and retrieve keys.

CLASSIC STRUCTURES & CLASSIC FREEDOMS

Entryway Priorities for *Classics*

- Purge at least annually if you live in a temperate climate, seasonally if you live somewhere horrible (like we do).
- Use bins and label the bejesus out of everything.
- Hide storage whenever physically possible.
- Don't be overly cost-conscious.
- Remember that having a clutter-free entryway is important for your sanity.
- Classic Structures: be considerate of others' possessions when you purge.
- Classic Freedoms: find alternate homes for sentimental items.

No, you really don't need two identical navy Brooks Brothers® overcoats

Get rid of coats first, because if you don't, your entryway will always be a mess. Purge with a vengeance: sell them, donate them, or as a last resort, if you're overwhelmed and they've sustained plenty of wear, throw them away (lower those eyebrows, we said it's a *last resort*, and most clothing is biodegradable). If you're a Classic Freedom who can't discard sentimental unworn coats, store them away. If your closet is still packed, then do seasonal change-outs or have alternate storage for infrequently worn items. If you have housemates, put your rejects in bags labeled with their destination and have family members go through them. Give a deadline. Classic Structures: it's technically unfair to get rid of other people's belongings without telling them. Just sayin'. After purging, you can rehang coats by type and season on your new matching wooden hangers.

All Classics are stressed out by clutter. But while a Classic Structure might have too many coats because he tends to be overly practical and keep good, unworn coats "just in case," a Classic Freedom might hold on to them because the one he bought right after college and doesn't wear anymore reminds him of "younger days." Classic Structures don't truly understand the sentimental-clothing-attachment thing.

Cubbies are dangerous

We know you're drawn to beautiful magazine images of open cubbies, but reality is messier. Open storage is a double-edged sword for you: it provides order, but then it invites clutter to hang out. Therefore, we only recommend open storage (cubbies, coat hooks with a bench underneath, or standing coat racks) if you have a back entrance, a true mudroom, or cubbies with doors, because otherwise the open storage will stress you out and compel you to constantly tidy it.

If no hidden-from-view scenario is possible, then install a rigid "One Coat, One Hook" policy, along with opaque bins that match the room's décor to hold other accessory detritus. Enforcing this rule is easiest if you are a Classic Structure, but it's totally possible for Classic Freedoms. Everyone would benefit from the one-hook, one-coat policy, but we'd only suggest it to you!

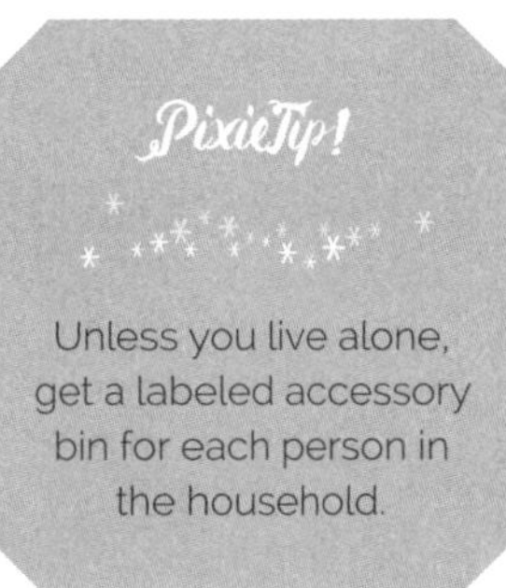

Behold: the Tao of tote bags

If our universal advice about five tote and paper shopping bags made the Classic Freedoms among you panic—*don't*. Unused sentimental bags can always go into storage, but make sure they're truly beloved. Revisit them in a year or two and see if you can let go. Alternatively, keep one favorite sentimental tote, get rid of nonmatching ones, and treat yourself to new ones that coordinate with it or colors in the closet or entryway. Nothing made Classic Freedom Kelly happier than when she got a shelf of matching L.L. Bean Boat and Tote® bags. We realize this will be hard for cost-conscious Classics, but once you replace your mishmash of bags with coordinating ones, the result will pay for itself in the daily Zen at your front door. After all, tote bags are not expensive when compared to college tuition or take-out food in New York City.

Gloves, scarves, and hats: oh, my!

Outerwear accessories multiply faster than coats for many reasons, such as "I got that in Paris" or "but I might find the missing glove one day." Follow our coat-purging advice for accessories, and then get deep, opaque, matching bins for each person and/or category. The more you delineate—e.g., summer hats/winter hats—the happier you'll be. Use labels. Avoid see-through and shallow bins. Before you ask: yes, color matters, even if these bins live inside a closet. Every time you open that closet door, those color-coordinated, matching bins will bring you satisfaction at a job well done in a way it won't for any other PixieType.

> **PixieTip!**
>
> Make sure there is extra room in the bins when you've filled them, or it'll be a jumbled mess two days after Jack Frost arrives.

You need just one row of shoes

Be discerning about what footwear you allow in your entryway. One row is perfection, two rows explains why your shoes need to be straightened twice a day, and three rows explains why it always looks like a mosh pit. Classic Freedoms: by now, you know what to do with any sentimental shoes. Try not to store things on the floor of an entryway closet, other than a few pairs of footwear (or kids' bins). It's difficult, but you will thank us when there's a magical PixieSpace for a return package. Any remaining shoes should be regularly transported to their proper homes in bedroom closets. But if that doesn't always happen, install one sturdy wooden shelf along the perimeter of the closet for excess shoes. Another idea for excess shoes is one or two color-coordinated hanging shoe compartments—assuming the shoe dirt next to your coats doesn't bug you (beware: the bags don't work well with men's shoes). Another option is to get a bench with space for opaque storage bins underneath, or place your shoes in large, deep opaque bins. Why? You'll be compelled to line up the shoes in an orderly, military-esque row if they're not hidden, and this is a colossal waste of your time on this planet!

Corral and hide paper, trash, and junk

Coats, mud, and sundry items are only part of the mess that entryways accumulate. The other part is mail, your papers, kids' papers, random objects, and packages. Make sure you have a designated *hidden* home for dumping things near your entrance, such as a console table with room underneath for various incoming objects. If these official homes don't exist, then the nearest available spot will become the default home. Try to prevent your dining table from being your dumping ground; a skinny console can fit almost anywhere.

Your household tray needs to be big enough to hold stuff until you have time to process the pile. If it gets too full too fast, put an identical one next to it or get a bigger tray. Ditto if random objects find their way there. If seeing a big pile of mail in your entryway tray bugs you, then hide it. Get a bin with a lid, a console with cabinet doors to hide inbox trays for every person in your home, or a bureau with drawers to serve as *or* hold inbox trays.

Another option is wall pockets like the ones you see holding magazines at doctors' offices—there are nice ones from Pottery Barn®—and install a wall hook for keys next to them. The drawback is that these bins are narrow, so only use them if you sort your mail frequently.

PixieTip!

Label your inboxes. Doing so will stop *most* people from putting random pieces of junk in there. Emphasis added on *most*, because there are always those in our midst who freely ignore labels.

If space is tight, get creative. One time we used an antique bureau with drawers as inboxes. Another time we put a small filing cabinet on wheels with a tray on top inside a client's entryway closet because she didn't have space for an extra table to house an inbox. Ah, the joys of NYC studios.

Tell others in the household what is and isn't allowed in the household inboxes, but know this will only be sporadically followed—people are tired when they come home. We like piles in trays because it's easier to put stuff away when it's corralled in an easy-to-transport place—say, when you're getting ready for guests. Note that a household inbox is just the first step; you also need a filing cabinet and a personal inbox for everyone who lives there. We discuss the rest of the system in Chapter 6: The Home Office (page 69).

Last but not least: recycle junk mail right where you sort through the mail. If you don't already have a receptacle, get one that works with the rest of the room's décor. We know you will carry the trash into the kitchen, but why make life harder for yourself? The kitchen trash isn't far, but it's an extra effort that those *less tidy than you* aren't necessarily going to make, leaving you with more work.

FUN STRUCTURES & FUN FREEDOMS

Entryway Priorities for *Funs*

- Purge at least annually, when the spirit moves you.
- Use bins and labels.
- Hide really ugly things.
- Handle bills, invites, and pressing items in the moment.
- Fun Structures: be considerate of others' stuff when you purge.
- Fun Freedoms: figure out how to let go of sentimental items.

Purge when you want to

Funs like things neat, tidy, and out of sight—much like Classics. However, you prefer to spend your time doing *fun* things rather than figuring out how to organize your closet. So let us do the work for you. Your entryway needs to have minimal clutter, order, hidden storage for ugly things, and your unique artistic touch. It also needs to be set up so that chores, like going through bills or hanging up coats, are practically done by themselves as you zoom through the front door.

If you never, ever, *ever* use the front door, then transform that front-hall closet into something else entirely, like a home office or utility or cleaning-supply closet.

If in doubt, throw it out!

If you're reading this, your closet is probably full of coats and stuff you've kept because either you're too busy to sort through them or you think they could come in handy one day. You are exceedingly practical and don't like to get rid of things that *could be* used, but these items take up precious space where actively used items should live instead. Putting it in your calendar to do seasonally just creates more work for you, so don't waste your time or mental energy writing lists when you've got one in your head already. When you do feel the urge to tackle this project, make sure it's a rainy day or one when you have nothing else going on. This activity will take you a while, and we don't want you to lose track of time, get halfway through, and have to rush off somewhere. We guess this tends to happen frequently, so trust us: give yourself the whole day, and we bet you'll be done by dinnertime. Get rid of enough coats and accessories to create empty hanging space. If anyone invented the forced deadline—like a party, or a visit from a judgmental relative—it was you, so use this tool to purge with a vengeance. Then get in the habit of throwing something out when you get something new, so you don't end up with a big, boring organization project on your hands *again*. The key for you to stay organized is to take care of things in the moment.

Fun Freedoms? Know that you're going to have a harder time getting rid of things than Fun Structures. Pare down how many souvenirs and categories you have in there. The coat closet should only hold coats, accessories, and shoes. If there's room, you can include another category or two, like bags or sports gear. If there isn't space for at least four extra hangers in the entryway closet, then you have more pruning to do. If there's a story behind something and you're loath to ditch it, put it in storage for a while. By the time you remember it, or have the time to look for it, you'll probably be able to let go.

Color-code your heart out

To the major annoyance of less motivated types, many of you guys won't throw anything out that you can make a buck on by selling or itemizing on your tax returns. Feel free to donate or sell what doesn't belong in your front hall, but while you're waiting for the urge to accomplish this task, give these items a temporary yet proper storage home, such as an attic, basement, or designated storage closet. Once you can see the back of the front-hall closet, get fastidious and hang coats by type—short, long, winter, spring/fall—or by color. You are seriously the only types who will get joy from color-coding and taking the time needed to maintain it.

Don't be a bag lady

If you couldn't whittle your tote-bag collection down to five quality, adored ones because a few were sentimental for you, then store them with your other sentimental items. All others should yield some price or brighten someone else's day.

Contain the jungle

Nope, you can't contain one in real life, but you can do it in your front-hall or back-door entrance. Use colorful, opaque bins for each category of outerwear accessories, with labels for gloves, hats, and scarves. Maybe different colors for different items or people? Do whatever floats your boat; you usually have an idea in mind that will please you far more than any diktat from us. (Plus, color-coding is your *thang.*) The best place for the bins is on the shelves above the coats. If you don't live alone and don't like the idea of people sharing your stuff—it's not OCD, just a proper respect for your own stuff—label accessory bins for each person in the household.

If you have a small, semi-hidden area off your entryway that you can turn into an actual mudroom with cubbyholes or lockers, this is ideal. It's nobody's dream scenario to stare at crusty, muddy boots when eating Cheerios® or after a long day's work. Ditto for standing coat racks. Use opaque bins inside cubbies, and label them so other people know what's inside. Yes, boxes inside boxes—we *know* you love them. Color code in here to your heart's content as well.

> **PixieTip!**
>
> Labels create a little more order, but, unlike some people, you don't need a label to remember what's there.

If you have tons of stuff that's not simple outerwear and only a basic closet in which to store it, then consider restructuring the whole shebang with a closet solution from The Container Store®, Home Depot®, or Lowe's®, mixing this other gear with regular closet stuff. You'd be amazed by what fits in a basic closet if you have the right infrastructure—the engineer in you will adore this solution. If you have to mix sports gear with coats and gloves, then you are going to have to be ruthless with your pruning.

Shoes are for clothes closets!

Only shoes, boots, kids' bins, or slippers (if you don't allow shoes in the house) should grace this closet floor. Keep it to one row of shoes, leaving space for those random items you're always dragging in the door. (Plus, if you don't have better things to do with your time than to straighten shoes every day, you're not a Fun!) If you have a very small closet and want floor space to keep bags out of sight, consider hanging shoe compartments, but remember: they're not great for men's shoes. You can also use a hanging sweater bin to store men's shoes, as well as excess sports and activity gear.

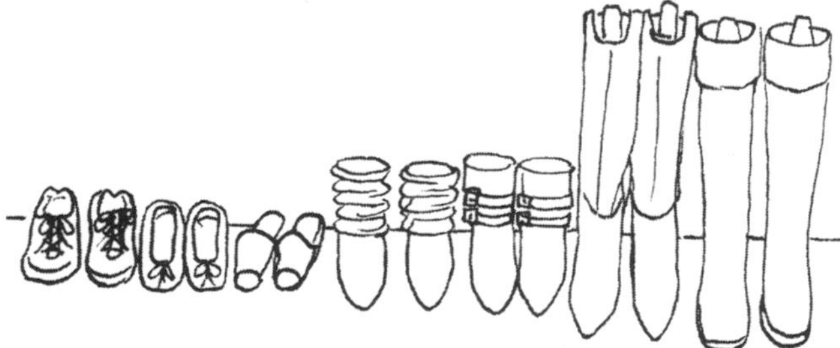

Maybe skip the paper/mail inbox

You need a designated surface for mail, papers, random objects, packages, etc. near your entrance to act as a landing pad, along with a household inbox so that others can grab their stuff. But if you're living solo, you might not need an actual inbox. When you plop mail into a tray to deal with later, things can linger in there for a while if you let them—a *long* while (okay for magazines, not for bills). So if no one else lives with you, then consider stuffing important mail in your bag/purse/briefcase to deal with when you've got the time and/or energy, wherever you are. Now, if you happen to have the time and energy right when you walk in the door, then go through it, take it to your home office, and sort it into your color-coded filing boxes.

ORGANIC STRUCTURES & SMART STRUCTURES

Entryway Priorities for
Organic Structures/Smart Structures

- Formalize entryway piles.
- Use transparent bins with labels.
- Make handling bills, invites, and pressing items a To-Do–list item.
- Keep household inbox in a high-traffic area.
- Purge annually, or have someone else do it.
- Smart Structures: inform people when you purge.
- Bring papers to your study or home office.
- Organic Structures: find new homes for sentimental items.

Other types divide and conquer; you need to formalize and contain!

If you don't have space for an entry table, use the next available surface where you wouldn't mind a pile or where you already naturally put stuff down. Some would say this is creating an illusion of order, but it's just you formalizing an already-existing solution that just happens to be unconventional. The inbox tray does just that. Own it. Seeing is remembering—especially for you—so this system works best if your inbox is in a high-traffic area. The visual reminder of that pile will scream "Remember to go through the mail!" Seeing a contained pile usually doesn't bother you the way it can bother other types, but if it does, you are hereby forewarned that if you let them move it to a low-traffic area or behind a cabinet door, you do so at your credit rating's peril! Instead, relocate the pile to your home office or wherever you go through your mail. This is step 1 in your new paper system. You'll also need more bins, not only for

> *PixieTip!*
>
> Get creative with your inbox: it can be anything, really, as long as it holds papers and packages. It could even be a drawer near the entryway, as long as you don't live with an Organic or a Smart.

other household members but also for your personal use, along with a filing cabinet. For detailed advice, see Chapter 6: The Home Office (page 69).

Another alternative for incoming paper is transparent acrylic wall pockets like those in doctors' offices for magazines. We gave this idea to one Organic Structure/Classic Structure pair who argued over their mail pile after they moved in together when he, the Classic, started putting their mail pile behind cabinet doors and she, the Organic Structure, started forgetting to pay the bills. (They ignored our advice and still argue about "The Pile" to this day.) Remember that whoever bears the ultimate responsibility for paying bills should win this inbox battle, for obvious reasons. Extrapolate this advice to other battles around the house: he who bears the brunt of the organizational task should be able to design the organizational solution, with some compromises.

If you leave things out as reminders to take them with you the following day, see if you can formalize this habit with an outbox (by this we mean a labeled, open, transparent tray placed on a surface in a high-traffic area near where you depart your home). Why? It will create more structure and, for Organic Structures, provide harmony by quieting a neatnik spouse who sees this habit as yet another messy pile. If the aforementioned neatnik complains about things hanging out in the outbox, then invite him/her to take on the chore of returning them.

Key hooks are for Classics

Any of the universal solutions for keys will work, but using a small ceramic or leather valet tray to drop your keys is best, as it's almost not even a step. You're going to release those keys from your grasp once you've opened your door, so you might as well do it over a bowl. Hanging your keys on a hook is a two-step process: first you find the key ring, then you hang it up. At first, Classic Kelly did not think of this as a two-step chore. It is!

Don't abuse coat racks; they're your friends

Moving on to garments, you should have a coat closet *and* a coat-hook rack near the most trafficked entrance, ideally. Be aware that coat racks not hidden from view will annoy detail-obsessed types, so if you live with one, coat racks are a potential battlefront (among many). Be careful with coat racks, as the bigger they are, the more you'll pile onto each hook, making it difficult to retrieve coats (plus, it looks terrible and often causes the rack to fall over). For you, anywhere that's aesthetically pleasing can serve as your mudroom.

PixieTip!

Please, please, please, *please* buy matching hangers. If you can't throw out existing ones, take a deep breath, put them in a box in storage, and see if you miss those awful wire and plastic tube hangers in a year.

Lots of organizers recommend taking pictures of sentimental items so that you can let go of the object but keep a visual reminder. In our experience, this works for maybe 10 percent of Organic Structures. The rest just roll their eyes.

For Organic Structures, anything can be sentimental

You need to get rid of a lot of outerwear—deep down, you already know this—and it is harder for Organic Structures to do so than it is for Smart Structures. We toyed with the idea of calling them "magpies" instead, because, left unchecked, the marriage of their practicality and sentimentality means they can accumulate enough stuff to be just shy of socially unacceptable. The easiest way to purge things is to not think about it. Start putting coats on your new wooden hangers and create the big picture before you deal with the details of purging specific items. We promise you'll get rid of things more easily this way. Post-purge, put those items that you don't use regularly but can't bear to discard into a box in an attic or extra closet. Revisit them next year, the year after, and so on, until you are able to let go or just accept that your storage room will always be a little fuller than your neighbor's. If it's still tight in your closet, make room in storage for seasonal change-outs.

You've got to see it to retrieve it

Next up, you need (no surprise) open, *transparent* bins for hats, gloves, scarves, and the like, so you can see what's inside. They have to slide easily in and out when placed on shelves. Label things if you live with others. If you or someone else ignores your new accessory organization system, at least you can see that this is happening before it gets out of hand.

> **PixieTip!**
>
> We know you're going to ignore our universal solution of keeping only five tote bags. If you do as we suspect, make sure that each bag has a proper home on a shelf or on a hook, and that you can easily retrieve each one. Next year, ask yourself if you used all of them. Repeat annually until you laugh when you realize just how right we were and how stubborn you are.

Oh, shoes

Now we tackle a waterloo for you and many others: shoes. The closet floor is priority seating for shoes and boots. We don't need to tell you that lining up shoes is a waste of your time on Earth. Shallow wide bins (six inches [15.2 cm] deep is perfect but twelve inches [30.5 cm] works, too) and whatever width works in the space—you've measured already, right?—are a great way to corral shoes in the bottom of a closet. These shoe bins can be *any* style you prefer—transparent *or* opaque—because you'll always be looking down on the contents. Remember, if the bins are too deep, you won't be able *to see* most of them. Also, a contrasting color will make them easier to see. Smarts: reserve a space in here for one or two nice pairs of shoes you don't want in the bins.

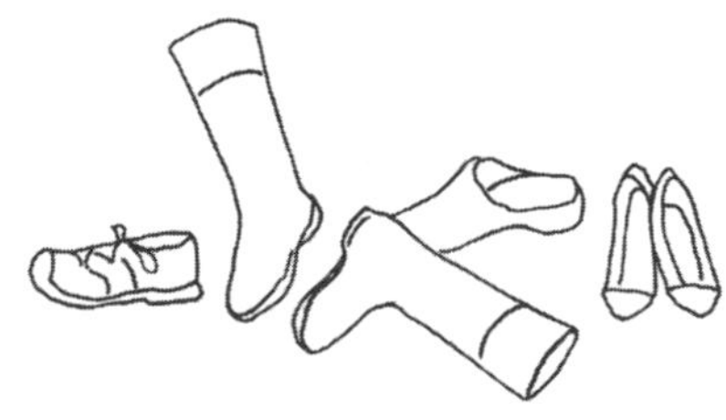

SMART FREEDOMS & ORGANIC FREEDOMS

Entryway Priorities for *Smart/Organic Freedoms*

- Formalize your natural unfurling habits.
- Purge when you have the impetus or mojo to do so.
- Try to do things in the moment.
- Have a junk drawer for last-minute tidying.
- Stretch your preferences and keep things like keys in the same place.
- Smart Freedoms: if you've never got the time or inclination to purge, then delegate it.
- Smart Freedoms: inform others when you purge.
- Organic Freedoms: find new homes for sentimental items.
- Know that while this is often a small part of your home, it's a tough one to keep tidy.

Create structure where you make a mess, unless it's your dining-room table

The reason entryways are tough for you is that, save for a stray baseball through a window, everything coming into or going out of your house—coats, hats, gloves, purses, luggage, paper, mail, and packages—goes through here, requiring hundreds of small decisions about where this or that should go. If you don't have the right systems in place to easily make those decisions when you're exhausted or in a hurry, then it starts to clutter up your doorway. Entryways can quickly become your worst nightmare: a Sisyphean struggle to achieve and maintain order!

The key to transforming your entryway and end-of-day habits is to reduce steps and eliminate decision-making. The easiest way to do this is to create structure around where you most often naturally dump things. If you don't put this new structure exactly where you dump, then you're going to keep dumping where you usually do, leaving you feeling guilty (if you're Organic) or annoyed (if you're Smart). Sure, it's easier if you dump all your gear in one place, but if you routinely hang on to your purse until you're in another room, or empty your pockets when you get undressed, don't change that habit: *formalize* it. Give your bag a formal home, deposit mail in a tray, give your wallet and keys a nice bowl, and if the miscellaneous objects and coins in your key container or wallet start bugging you, dump them into a designated junk drawer. Junk drawers are not an admission of organizational defeat but an unconventional, necessary solution: you'll always know where to look for errant business cards, important receipts, and random doodads you never knew where to put before.

> **PixieTip!**
>
> Caveat: While nobody should use a dining table or kitchen counter as their dumping ground—it inhibits their designated purposes—for you it's *extra* important, because your dumping is messier and longer-lasting than others'. As an alternative, create a surface as close to this area as possible.
>
> Every once in a while—like when you haven't seen the wall in months, or have trouble squeezing by the massive wall mound—remove less-used or off-season coats from your hooks and store them on hangers in the closet.
>
> We know you often leave umbrellas wherever you were when it stopped raining (porch, doctor's office, car, etc.), so keep a supply of cheap ones on hand in a bin, and leave your roommate's nice ones alone!

Hooks will be your saving grace

Next, take off your coat and shoes and stay a while, then go to the closet and hang up your coat on a hanger *if* this is your current ritual. But, if you tend to drape your coat and sundries on the nearest chair, then use hooks. There's no shame in not hanging up your coat on a hanger. It's a friggin' five-step process, and multistep organization is your kryptonite. Hooks on a wall are a one-step solution; hooks inside the closet are two steps. If your entryway is formal, then do the latter. Otherwise, mount the hooks outside the closet—just make sure that you or others in your home don't hate seeing that jumble of coats every day (it will annoy most types to some degree, but if this system is in a back hallway, along with a bench, bins, and/or a row of cubbyholes, most people can deal with it).

But no key hooks for you!

You do best using a small attractive bowl or tray for keys in the entranceway near your natural dumping ground—or tucking them in your purse or coat pocket, assuming you use the same one most days—as it's easier to drop or tuck and retrieve than to use the two-step hook process. Tiny, random things and coins will eventually find their way into this bowl, to the point where it's almost a junk bowl, but this shouldn't bug you too much, as now you have a coin bowl! (If it does, get another bowl for keys. And do you remember that hidden junk drawer we mentioned? Use it. Dump those bits and bobs in there or in the trash.)

Purge and conquer!

Now, stay with us for a moment. Imagine getting home and finding a hanger, and then struggling to hang your coat back in a closet that's bursting at the gills. Yeah, we know: it's not exactly tempting to repeat this valiant effort. If that's what your front-hall closet looks like, then—when you can't stand it anymore—clear that puppy out. Don't focus on purging; focus on *organizing*. As you try to implement our universal solutions from the previous pages and some of our organizing ideas on the next pages, you'll soon notice that there are tons of low-hanging fruit to get rid of. When you've reached purging altitude, you'll be in a zone, at which point we suggest purging everything (coats, hats, gloves, scarves, bowling balls, tennis rackets, etc.) you can stand to part with—unless you want to go through this again in twelve months. With you guys, stuff can accumulate to just shy of that socially unacceptable level because you're not one to spend free time thinking about possessions to throw out (as other "alien" people do).

If there are things you can't part with for various reasons, store them in a box in the attic or another storage space. Label and date it. As you know, out of sight is out of mind, so when you "rediscover" these items after you purge your attic—which will eventually have turned into a polite hoarder's nest—you'll know what you can get rid of or bring back into rotation. Don't overthink where to donate; just find a local donation place that's on your daily route. *Convenience* is the key to success. If taking clothes to a recycling center proves too much, throwing out clothes is an absolute last resort (nobody wants to be the one who contributes to the landfill, but you also don't want to be the one living in a landfill, either).

> **PixieTip!**
>
> Only keep tote bags that you actually find yourself using in a pinch. Store sentimental ones elsewhere and get rid of them when you forget you still have them. Only keep three to five of those fancy-paper shopping bags.

Hats and gloves go in transparent bins on the shelf above the coats—or stuff 'em in your coat pockets, where you'll magically find them after thinking you've forgotten them at home.

Shoes, shoes, shoes!

Okay, here is the perennial question you've probably never asked yourself unless it was raining and your shoes were soaked: Should I take off my shoes here? The answer is *yes*, because otherwise you're going to shed them wherever you are when they start bothering you, and you might forget where that is. Try to kick your shoes off here, in a bin that's not deeper than six to twelve inches (15–31 cm), and grab a pair of slippers or socks if your feet are cold. If the bin is deeper than that, you won't find the shoes you want come morning. You'll probably have to clear this bin out from time to time and take shoes back to your room when it *overfloweth*, but if you only have your shoes in two places, the chances of wildly running around your house trying to find them when you needed to be out the door five minutes ago are slim.

Mail can't wait

Many types can just leave mail in their household inbox to deal with later. You can't. Sorry, but the evidence and research is clear on your type: if you don't take care of it right away, before or right after you take off your coat, it will be there a week or a month later when you're looking for those curriculum-night details or that IRS letter in an unwieldy pile. The trick to staying organized is to set up things so you can do tasks the minute they present themselves. You really only need an inbox if you're living with a Classic, Organic Structure, or Smart Structure who wants one.

Sort your mail into these categories: "Catalogs/Magazines," "Bills," "Junk Mail," "Things for Your Calendar," "Other Things to File," and "Other People's Mail." If you already have an entryway tray, then you can technically keep catalogs and magazines in there, but it's not the ideal solution, as they'll likely collect dust in this location. You're better off if you pile them somewhere you might read them, like the bathroom or coffee table. Bills and "Other Things to File" should come with you to the home office (or remain in the tray, if that's your home office). If magazines live in that tray, then get a second tray. Junk mail goes straight into a wastebasket you've put right where you go through the mail. Stash "Things for Your Calendar" in your bag for later input into the computer, phone, or organizer. If you feel like doing it right away, go ahead, but this category can wait until you've decompressed or have some extra time. The genius of keeping the calendar stuff in your bag, purse, or coat pocket is that when you're ready to go through it, it's by your side. Other people's mail can sit in the household inbox awaiting their perusal. See Chapter 6: The Home Office (page 69) for more on your new paper system.

Entryway Checklist

- ☐ Decluttered front-hall closet or mudroom
- ☐ Donated coats, totes, and sundries to charity
- ☐ Sold higher-value items
- ☐ Found temporary, appropriate homes for things you can't donate or sell right now
- ☐ Measured every square inch of the entryway/closet
- ☐ Bought personality-appropriate bins for accessories and shoes
- ☐ Bought matching hangers
- ☐ Got an entryway tray (if applicable)
- ☐ Communicated with other household members on the new system for outerwear and paper
- ☐ Labeled everything (unless you're an Organic, a Smart, or a Fun who lives alone)
- ☐ Hung up your coat and put away everything in its place, every day for a week. Rocking!

CHAPTER SIX

The Home Office

If you're over ten years old, you need a home office. Make no mistake: a household is a business operation; the business is your life. Most of us are not running the equivalent of Downton Abbey or the White House, but there still needs to be a place where you manage and store the nuts and bolts. A home office doesn't have to be an entire room. It's just the place—desk, cabinet, or room—where you go through your mail and attend to the demands in your life. The only place it can't be situated is your dining room, because breaking bread alongside a tax return appeals to no one, and you will stop using your dining room for its intended purpose—i.e., eating with friends and family in good cheer (give or take a few awkward or awful meals that we all try to forget with our Norman Rockwell–esque hazy memories).

UNIVERSAL SOLUTIONS

Home-Office Essentials for *All Types*

- Create a quasi-mailroom, with inboxes for every household member.
- Implement a document storage system.
- Labels are a "must" in multiperson households.
- Throw out nonessential papers.
- Have a wastebasket or shredder nearby.
- Communicate your new system to everyone.

Create a quasi-mailroom

Our instinct with home offices is to re-create what we do in our workplace office, and while this works for some—if that's you, great!—it's a disaster for others. There are, however, two staples of every office that everyone needs to re-create in some form. First: the mailroom. If you're in charge of running a multiple-person household, regardless of who you are, it's easiest if everyone has their own personal inbox. This is where paper and mail—along with things that don't have an obvious home—are stored. Think of it as a temporary holding bin. Get bins large and deep enough to handle different sizes of paper and items.

Remember, whoever is in charge of this quasi-mailroom is the de facto office manager. It's likely you, since you're reading this book, which means you've got to make sure other people in the household understand the system you create.

Implement a document-storage system

The second office staple everyone needs to re-create is a paper/document storage system. Remember, home filing systems should vary widely, based on your PixieType. But when it comes to the "old school" filing cabinet, there is one tip that's good for multiple PixieTypes: Classic Freedoms, Fun Freedoms, and Organics remember files more easily when they have nonspecific labels reflecting how they think or feel about them (e.g., "Tax Stuff 2013," *not* "Federal Tax Form 1040-2013" or "Federal Deductions 2013"). One of our Fun Freedom clients had a file that held all the parking tickets she'd fought and won, named "The Man" instead of "Parking Tickets." She knew exactly what was in that file, even though the label wasn't specific or logical.

Everyone else can use alphabetical no-nonsense logic when filing, though.

Yes, all PixieTypes must label

If you live with others, then you need to know where your stuff is if you didn't sort it. The more categories that are labeled, the less likely you are to start a new pile on the kitchen table. Yes, all types have done and will do this if there isn't a labeled "miscellaneous" bin or file.

You don't need your cable bill from 2015

Everybody has too many papers in their current filing system. Remember: you only have to keep documents that you might need again one day. Tax receipts and returns generally don't have to go back further than seven years. Bills and statements don't need to hang around for more than twelve months. Instead, keep your end-of-year statements. If you fear the federal Tax Man—as you should!—then once the tax year is done, store those receipts and tax-preparation stuff in a deep storage area, like the basement or attic. It doesn't need to be in your active office, especially if you're short on space. Don't forget to have a wastebasket or shredder right where you go through papers.

PixieTip!

Have trouble keeping necessary receipts? Use a gallon-size Ziploc® bag marked "Receipts 2016." It's easy to stuff receipts from a wallet in there, and it takes a while to fill up. (No worries about their getting wet, either—is there any dilemma a Ziploc bag doesn't solve?).

If you've got sentimental correspondence that you want to keep, files aren't the best place for them. Instead, get a large labeled bin for each person in the household, where these items can go to stay forever (before most of them are thrown away one day).

Explain your new system to the entire household (or it will fail)

All your good work in organizing this fabulous new household mailroom/home office will be for naught if you don't tell everyone about it. Labels don't explain the rhyme and reason behind the system, and nothing will change unless you take everyone aside separately or hold a big family meeting. In fact, this is true of all organizational changes you make to a home. Sing it from the mountaintop loud and clear, and don't get discouraged if your soldiers don't fall into line right away. New routines take at least three months to become ingrained (and that's really just true for Classics). There are rebels among the PixieTypes, so communicate how important this new system is and how adhering to it is a way for them to show their love and appreciation for your efforts. If that doesn't work? Go all General MacArthur on their you-know-whats, and they'll fall in line soon enough.

CLASSIC STRUCTURES & CLASSIC FREEDOMS

Home-Office Priorities for *Classics*

- Replicate a typical workplace office, but match it to your home's décor.
- Have individual inboxes for everyone, unless you live alone.
- To-Do lists and calendars are your lifeblood.
- Purge annually.
- Let others know when their inboxes are going to be emptied for them.

Organize your office the way you do at work—only nicer

You are the PixieTypes that can and should replicate everything in a typical workplace office at home. That includes an inbox, an outbox, a calendar, a To-Do list, a physical desk, a filing cabinet, a printer, and drawers with organizer bins for office supplies. Forget the ugly cubicle walls, and go beyond using an old, unloved coffee mug to store pens or some generic pen holder. Instead, coordinate the office with the rest of your décor. File cabinets don't have to be black, gray, or tan. Get an attractive one instead that has more room than you currently need, because even with pruning, files always multiply. Attractive office supplies and furnishings may seem trivial, but, in the end, they're worth it. If you take the time to decorate your office the way you would any other room in the house, you'll be happier day-to-day as you deal with running your household.

Have individual inboxes for everyone, unless you live alone

Your entryway inbox can serve as your personal inbox, unless there are more people than just you in the household. In the latter case, create a household mailroom. As for your personal inbox, if you find that you have paper that's not ready to be filed nor thrown away while sorting through it, then you probably need an interim box—a holding pen for papers in process—but you'll be happier if you can avoid this by getting into a routine of regularly going through your stuff one to three times a month, depending on needs. Put your new routine on your To-Do list until it's an ingrained habit.

Hide office items away in drawers or behind cabinet doors, with labels inside and drawer organizers to hold loose items—especially if your home office isn't a separate room. You don't need to see the riffraff to know it's there, and clearer work surfaces will give you more peace of mind.

To-Do lists and calendars are your lifeblood

You are the best PixieTypes for maintaining routines. Almost all of you use a daily To-Do list and calendar because it's the difference between feeling powerful and powerless. Taking the time every day to evaluate priorities and fitting things in your schedule helps you see the big picture more easily. Use electronic or handwritten calendars and To-Do lists—whatever works best. If you're not getting something done on your precious list, break it down into steps. You'll soon get to cross it off your list (which you do religiously after you finish something).

Home Office

1 Piles happen no matter what your type when their contents have no homes.

2 Bank boxes are a jerry-rigged solution; papers need permanent, attractive homes.

3 These old-school file cabinets should be banned from all homes across the globe.

4 Beware the over-burdened bulletin board.

5 Desktop computers don't actually have to be kept on precious desktop space.

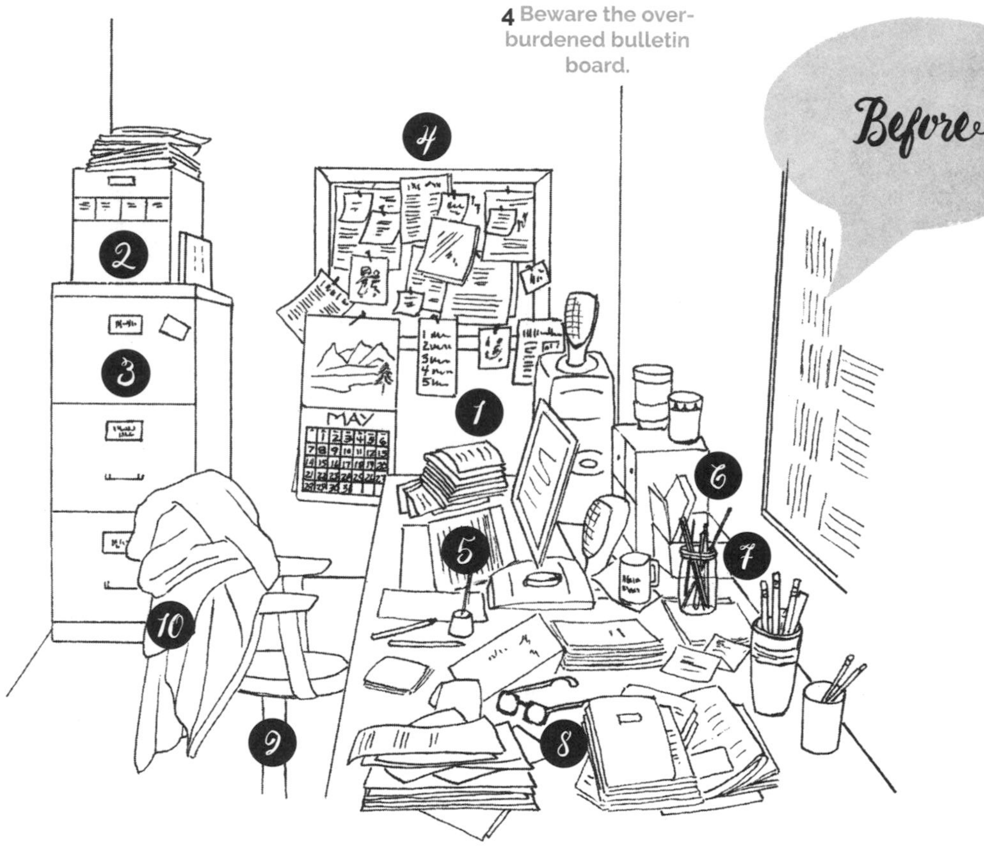

6 Here we have a random organizer that's never used because it's hidden beneath the mess.

7 Mismatched pens and pen corrals (hint: they just add to the mess).

8 Three more piles of papers. Hmm . . . perhaps we've got an Organic or Smart here.

9 Here's an ugly office chair. Maybe that's why there's always a coat draped on it.

10 This home office is crying out for some hooks to hang this coat on!

1 Ah, a hook!

2 Here's a nice home for the printer, with paper conveniently stored above.

3 Classics and Funs need a cabinet to hide stuff in. If an Organic or Smart lives with a Classic or Fun, they can hide their presorted piles here.

4 An Organic's and Smart's presorted piles need to be contained in translucent bins. These bins are half the height of the bookshelf and labeled so others can use them if need be.

5 An accordion file holder is great for an Organic or Smart's active files (items not ready for deep storage).

6 Bookshelves are for books and are essential for Smart Structures and other book lovers.

7 If you're an Organic or a Smart, file cabinets are for deep storage only.

8 Life is just too short not to invest in attractive, lateral filing cabinets.

9 Use this space to feature a beautiful and comfortable office chair (which can also be used as extra seating in the dining room).

10 Drawers! Just what was needed—a place to hide pens and other office supplies . . . and maybe a junk drawer for Organics and Smarts.

11 A well-curated bulletin board.

Purge annually

When you're filing papers, make sure they are things you will need again one day. (If you don't know the answer, Google® it—duh.) Harness the power of your detail-orientedness to figure out the minutiae instead of wondering. Set aside time once a year to go through your filing cabinet and throw things away (good times are often the week between Christmas and New Year's, right before school starts, or the beginning of spring). Put it in your calendar. You are awesome at purging once you get a routine going.

> *PixieTip!*
>
> Take the time to alphabetize your files, as it'll be a lot easier to find anything at any time.

Let others know when their inboxes are going to be emptied for them

You can try to get others to follow your habits, but managing people at home is even harder than managing people in the office. It's like herding cats. Give fair warning when someone else's inbox is getting unruly and you're about to lose your temper and throw things away or move them to a different area of the house.

FUN FREEDOMS & FUN STRUCTURES

Home-Office Priorities for *Funs*

- You can replicate a workplace office, as long as it looks good.
- Inboxes are necessary for others, but not for you.
- You don't need written To-Do Lists.
- Get more file storage than you need, so you only have to go through it when you feel like it.

Replicate a workplace office, only less boring

Like Classics, you guys do well replicating a typical office at home—a physical desk, a filing cabinet, a printer, paper, and drawers with organizer bins for office supplies—and if you buy décor with more *joie de vivre* than your average boring office, you might hate the drudgery of running a household a little less. If a few unattractive office items end up in your midst, just hide them in drawers or cabinets with labels and drawer organizers to hold loose items.

PixieTip!

Accordion file boxes are a wonderful solution for you, especially if they have a handle so you can bring them with you when you've got a long wait at the doctor's office, a long train commute, and the like.

Avoid a household inbox, if you can

The first caveat to replicating an office at home is to avoid a household inbox if possible—it's like paper purgatory for you. Instead of dropping things in an inbox, either deal with papers immediately—put things in your calendar, write checks, shuffle items into your filing cabinet or other people's inboxes in your quasi-mailroom—or keep papers that need immediate action in your bag so you can do things when you've got the time or energy. Remember, your strength is dealing with things in the moment. There's no time like the present, and if that's not possible, create a scenario where you can get it done anywhere, anytime. We have one Fun client who carries office supplies in her purse, which is essentially a roving office.

You don't need written To-Do lists

The second caveat to replicating an office at home is that you don't need written To-Do lists. Funs can often be accused of being scatterbrained and have often been told that To-Do lists are necessary to stay organized. By all means, keep a calendar, but since your To-Do lists are already in your head, writing them down is generally a tedious and unnecessary step. A better way for you to remember to do things is to set reminder alarms on your phone, send yourself an e-mail, or do like Katie and Richard Branson and write a reminder on your hand. Jotting one down is a last resort, if you've got too much on your plate.

Get more file storage than you need

Store papers in an attractive file cabinet, file boxes, or portable accordion file boxes. We know it's an extra expense, and you like to be practical, but life is too short to stare at ugly filing units. It's key for you to have more storage room in file boxes and cabinets than you need—buy extra so you don't have to prune files yearly. Yes, you *should* do it yearly, but you probably won't. This gives you the freedom to purge paper when you're inspired to do it rather than because your inbox is stuffed to the gills. If you're in doubt about paper, Google whether there's a reason to keep it, and if there's not, chuck it. One Fun client asks herself whether it's something a loved one will just throw out when she dies. It's grim, but hey—don't knock it 'til you try it.

ORGANIC STRUCTURES & SMART STRUCTURES

Home-Office Priorities for *Organic/Smart Structures*

- Use contained piles and/or metal accordion file racks to keep track of active projects.
- Filing cabinets are for long-term storage only.
- Sort through your inbox on a monthly basis.
- Use a calendar and To-Do list to remind yourself of what needs to get done and when.
- Bulletin boards are useful, but prune them regularly.

Pile to your heart's content . . . neatly

You don't have to replicate an office at home to successfully manage your affairs. Don't get us wrong—you'll need the basics: master calendar, office supplies, printer, paper, etc.—but your setup can be less traditional. Find a place for a bookshelf or credenza near your desk—or in place of a traditional desk—for piles held in labeled, transparent bins. As for why it doesn't work to pile things without structure: labeled, transparent bins for piles let the outside world know these are purposeful piles, so they're more likely to be treated with respect.

We had an Organic Structure client who initially just had a few random piles on her desk. Now she has an entryway pile in a basket, an "in process" pile in an open transparent bin, a "catalog" pile in a basket nearby, along with an "important paper" pile and a "to file" pile. Your piles will likely differ, but you get the gist. As piles fill up their bins, they serve as a visual reminder to go through and decide what needs to be dumped and what needs to be saved.

Filing cabinets aren't for active projects

Using piles in a formal way is a substitute for using an active filing cabinet. It's not that you can't use a filing cabinet or vaguely remember what's in there, but why use it if you don't have to? Store things in here that you don't need

PixieTip!

If you've got a lot of in-progress papers, an open desktop accordion/step/tiered file sorter is a great tool, as it gives you even more visual certainty about where each project is. Another solution is to use big clips to delineate different projects in a pile.

to access daily or weekly: insurance policies, wills, dental records, and so on. Keep it in the home office—or elsewhere, if you lack the space.

Sort through your inbox monthly

A household inbox is a great initial pile in which to drop papers and mail, even if you're living alone. Use this pile to feed other piles once or twice a month, depending on what's going on in your household. Put this task on your master calendar to get it done. Once sorting through this initial pile is routine, you can probably leave it off your To-Do list. As you're going through your pile, input To Dos from the piles into your calendar.

Use a calendar and To-Do list

If you don't have a calendar and a To-Do list—electronic or paper—this needs to be remedied ASAP. Even if you've acquiesced to the electronic version, a paper To-Do list often works better for you, as it doesn't get lost on a phone or computer screen between countless folder and application icons. You see the big picture better than most PixieTypes, but there's something about writing things down that helps you remember them better than you would otherwise—perhaps because you don't see things in your head as easily as Funs, Organic Freedoms, and Smart Freedoms.

Bulletin boards are useful, but they can get unruly

You are drawn to bulletin boards because of their visual impact, but you'd better be good at pruning them. Small items you tend to forget about—key receipts, invitations, or gift cards—are great to stick up there, as are wall calendars—nothing beats visually seeing your day or month in front of you. If you like using Post-It® notes to remind yourself of things, you can pin these on the bulletin board and it'll give these little pieces of paper more permanence. You guys might have more bits of paper than the next person, but you don't like a mess, so add pruning the bulletin board to your To-Do list.

ORGANIC FREEDOMS & SMART FREEDOMS

Home-Office Priorities for *Organic/Smart Freedoms*

- It's all about the piles.
- File cabinets are mausoleums, where paper goes to die.
- Create predetermined piles so you don't need to make decisions about where to put papers.
- Throw stuff out when you're looking for something else.
- To-Do lists? Fuhgeddaboudit! (Unless you are overwhelmed with too many tasks.)

It's all about the piles

In no way, shape, or form do you have to re-create a typical office at home. In fact, don't. It's a waste of time and space. You're not usually the type of person who wants to work at the same desk day after day, anyway. But you do need a central spot for the piles that pertain to running your household. This spot needs many open surfaces for piles in labeled, transparent bins. They can be bookshelves, a beautiful table or desk, or even shelves in a cabinet (although hidden piles are never ideal). If a cabinet is all you have or it's in your entryway, it'll work—as long as you have some other open surface for a few key piles in open, transparent bins.

File cabinets are mausoleums where paper goes to die

Don't use a household inbox if you can help it; it's paper purgatory for you and can quickly become paper hell. When you come home, deal with papers right away or keep items that need immediate action in your bag, so you can do things when you've got the time or energy. For you, a file cabinet is a mausoleum: you close the doors and forget what's in there, making retrieval very difficult. Therefore, never, ever file something away that you might want to work on in the next five to twenty years.

Creating predetermined piles removes the need to use your brain

One of your stumbling blocks with paper is deciding where to put it. This can be debilitating, so you decide to figure it out later and put paper in a big miscellaneous pile that used to be called your desk. Our advice is to have predetermined piles that replace your useless filing cabinet. As to figuring out what types of piles to have, conduct an archaeological dig on your existing piles. Sort through the papers, putting like with like, and when you're done, your pile categories will materialize (e.g., "bills," "medical reimbursements," "kids' stuff," "invites," "catalogs," "to read"). Once you have settled on categories, you have a rough draft of your filing system. Keep in mind that it is only a rough draft, and get a few extra bins to have on hand. It's an iterative process, but one of your strengths is being Zen with process, so go with it.

> **PixieTip!**
>
> You do your best work in the moment when you're inspired. Whenever you postpone something boring, there's maybe a 50/50 chance you'll actually ever get to it, depending on the level of importance. If something is boring? Invent a new way to be inspired, like a paint project or new organizing gear, and it will get done.

Throw stuff out when you're looking for something else

Even though you'll likely have lots of bins, they will eventually overflow to the point where you're compelled to go through them and throw things away or put them in their final resting place (aka your filing cabinet). But say you're going through the piles to get something you need, and you notice other stuff that can be thrown out. Should you? Yes.

To-Do lists? Fuhgeddaboudit! (Unless . . .)

Almost every human has a calendar, and if it helps you, then—by all means—keep one. Just remember: it won't be even close to foolproof for you. Use electronic reminders with alarms for important meetings and events. E-mail yourself reminders for important To Dos. When you've got a lot on your plate and are worried about forgetting stuff, then To-Do lists are like a data dump. (You're not the kind to obsessively cross things off your list because, well, you forget.) We have one Organic Freedom client who makes To-Do lists when she's stressed out and doing too much, another who uses them just for work. She makes one list and then never refers to it again, but whenever she comes across one a few years later, she always laughs when she realizes she accomplished everything on that list without referring to it more than once. Ditto for our client who uses them just at work.

Home Office Checklist

- ☐ Found an appropriate home* for your home office
- ☐ Decluttered existing piles, and/or file cabinets
- ☐ Measured every square inch of office space/room
- ☐ Bought all necessary (attractive!) office furnishings and supplies
- ☐ Bought bins to label for each member of your household and created a quasi-mailroom
- ☐ Communicated with other household members about the new paper-handling system
- ☐ Got your boring home-office duties done and found everything you needed for one month

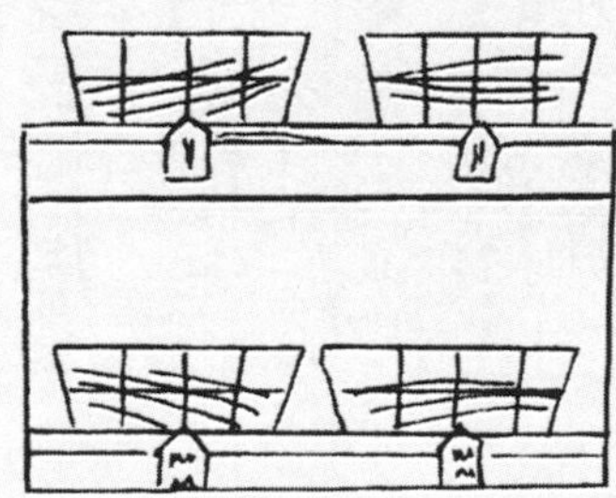

*Appropriate home = not your dining room or kids' room. We saw someone using his kids' bedroom as an office on TV recently. *Bad idea.*

CHAPTER SEVEN

The Kitchen

The kitchen is the central gathering place in most homes (everybody's gotta eat!). Therefore, solutions have to work for all personality types . . . or chaos will ensue. Much of our advice for this room is universal, and it's where labeling comes in most handy, since what's obvious to you isn't always obvious to your spouse or mother-in-law. As with any disorganized area, there's too much stuff in the kitchen, but there are three major areas everyone can focus their purging efforts on to make this area tidier: spices, coffee mugs, and pot lids. We've come across just one exception to this rule in the past nine years: a Classic stay-at-home mom with a full-time nanny *and* a cleaning lady, because that's the trifecta it takes to have a consistently perfect kitchen!

UNIVERSAL SOLUTIONS

Kitchen Essentials for *All Types*

- Purge!
- Matching containers aren't a necessity.
- Measure everything.
- Store dishware near the dishwasher.
- Adjust cabinet shelves for maximum efficiency.
- Use cabinet organizers, lazy Susans, and drawer bins.
- Label.
- Your fridge is not a bulletin board.
- Make grocery lists.
- Cleaning products go in a caddy.
- Plastic grocery bags need a formal home.
- Use the magical "Later Box" if you can't part with stuff.

Spices and coffee mugs are like gremlins: they multiply when you're not looking

We've yet to come across an actively used kitchen where the client hasn't had an army of spices taking over the pantry. Purging spices is an easy project that you can finish in under an hour. Spices expire, and unless you're a professional cook, you don't need multiple bottles of cumin. Go through the rest of your pantry, too, because canned goods and other nonperishables go bad; they only last for five years.

Check "Best by" dates and chuck what's past its prime or donate what will be by the time you get around to eating it. While these aren't actual expiration dates, food banks will not accept food past these dates, so why should *you*?

And we've never met a kitchen that didn't have an overflowing mishmash of sentimental mugs from alma maters and Timbuktu. Of course, you can keep those you use (duh), but chuck the rest or use them elsewhere if you can't let go. Ditto for all tableware and flatware. Kelly keeps her childhood Cinderella cup in her bedroom as a place to store her makeup brushes. If you have a full set of everything, then you don't need to hang on to the three salad plates or forks left over from your grandmother's. Also, you don't have to start afresh if you're missing pieces—see if they sell your patterns on www.replacements.com. As for cooking utensils, get rid of duplicates or useless ones that just make it harder to find the things you *do* use—carrot curlers, special strawberry cutters, etc.—and keep the best ones. As for knives, if they don't cut well and can't be professionally sharpened, they're pointless in the kitchen other than moonlighting as weapons.

Rethink the matching containers

The next time you see an enviable pantry on Pinterest® with all of the cereals and grains dutifully poured into matching sealed containers, remember that this involves extra work every time you grocery-shop. Somebody has to pour things into those containers week after week. If it's worth it to you, then go for it. Otherwise, save yourself the hassle.

Measure EVERYTHING

We learned this the hard way when we first started out. Almost everything would fit, except for *one* thing. Nothing kills an organizing project like being unable to finish because you bought the wrong-size items. Before you shop, measure the depth, height, and width of even the smallest crevice.

PixieTip!

Everyone holds on to plastic food containers. Ditch mismatched bottom/tops or stained ones. Takeout containers aren't designed for continued use. When you heat them to the level they need to get clean, the plastic degrades and leaches into food. Recycle these, then upgrade.

Efficiency matters

Store glasses, dinnerware, flatware, and cooking utensils close to the dish-washer, where they will be easiest to unload. Stand by the dishwasher with the door open, pretend to unload it, and you'll quickly figure out the most efficient configuration. It's what we do when we're helping clients move into new homes or notice an awkward kitchen layout.

Adjust cabinet shelves

PixieTip!

If you're short on space, make sure everything stored in the kitchen *needs* to be stored there. (For example, a slow cooker used two times a year doesn't need to be *in* the kitchen all the time.)

Organizing kitchen cabinets is like doing a giant movable jigsaw puzzle, but it's necessary. Don't be afraid to change the level of shelves to maximize vertical space, but avoid stacking different sizes of plates on top of each other. Cabinet risers exist so you don't have to lift off the salad plates every time you want a dinner plate. Ditto for stacking cups on top of each other—too many steps. Sometimes you need to adjust shelves a few times while trying different sizes of shelf risers until everything fits perfectly. It takes *a lot* of patience to get it right, and one cup can throw it all off. (It's no wonder Kelly's husband's freebie travel mugs from conferences always seem to "mysteriously" disappear.)

Retrieving items in lower cabinets is incredibly easy when you install pullout shelves. They're perfect for pots and pans (less bending over and reaching). You can get premanufactured ones or cheap, customizable ones that are easy to install by yourself. On these movable shelves, corral small, loose pantry items that don't stack well into small, open, transparent bins. Ditto for small boxes of pasta, cereal, or rice.

Make retrieval easier with organizers, lazy Susans, and bins

Pot lids don't have to be monogamous. Make sure there's a pot for every lid, then get rid of extraneous ones that are the same size and could service multiple pots and pans. As for storing them, buy pot-lid organizers to keep lids separate from the pots because you don't need a lid *every* time you need a pot. Avoid stacking pots and pans more than three high, as this makes what is a two-step process—open cupboard door, grab pot—into three, four, or five steps.

Lazy Susans work wonders for narrow items (e.g., cans, spices) in upper and lower cabinets. What you lose in free space, you gain in the ease of retrieving items at a moment's twirl and glance. Transparent cabinet bins are also helpful for things like soup packets, nuts, candy, and drink mixes.

Another area of common cabinet disorganization is cutting boards, cookie sheets, and baking pans. There's usually a narrow cupboard designed for these tall, cumbersome items. Installing an internal organizer for this space is easy—we're talking two small screws. Even shelf dividers meant for clothes—no screws needed—can work if there's a shelf.

In shallow kitchen drawers, use smaller bins to separate cutlery *as well as* cooking utensils. Drawers are also great storage spaces for wraps and foils, not to mention junk. Random crap finds its way into kitchens, but if it's corralled in a drawer, the rest of your kitchen remains better organized. If you can't waste a full drawer on junk, at least reserve a drawer bin.

Label things in common areas

We remember making fun of the owner of a beach rental who had labeled everything in the kitchen, down to the spoons. But after ten years of organizing kitchens, we now know better. If you want your organized kitchen to stay organized when sharing it with others, then you need to label basic categories—plate locations (salad vs. dinner), bowls, cups, mugs, as well as pantry items such as grains/pastas, canned goods, cereal—or communicate where everything goes. Absent one or the other, you can't expect people to perfectly maintain your kitchen. Organics and Smarts: We know you'll resist labeling, but if someone in your household is driving you nuts putting spoons where the knives go, then save some breath and point to the knife label on the container filled with spoons.

PixieTip!

Unlabeled bins become junk bins. Kelly kept one for leftover candy. It seemed obvious, yet she continued to find dried fruit and nuts in there. She told her husband what the bin was for, slapped a label on it, and finally: no random stuff.

Your fridge is not actually a bulletin board

Everyone can do with a bulletin board in a well-trod space—if space allows—to catch the clutter that inevitably ends up under magnets on the fridge, such as kids' artwork and invitations. Fridge doors are not ideal places for these things, because people are constantly opening and closing them, which causes items to fall off. The bulletin board gives a structure and purpose to papers meant for all to see, the same way the lazy Susan does with cooking condiments near the stove.

Make grocery shopping easier—write it down

Keep a running grocery list on your fridge or nearby on a pad of paper. If you jot it down whenever you are running low on something, you'll waste less time going through your fridge and pantry before every trip to the grocery store. *But*—isn't there always a *but*?—make sure others in your household buy into this idea, because if they're not jotting things down, then the list will never be accurate, and you'll still have to take stock of what you have before every grocery trip.

Keep a cleaning caddy

Corralling kitchen cleaning supplies in a transportable caddy under your sink makes it easier for you and others to retrieve multiple items in close to one step when it's time to scrub the stovetop and wipe down the counter. (If you have young children, though, cleaning supplies should be stored out of reach for safety reasons.)

Plastic grocery bags will survive the apocalypse

Plastic grocery bags are the bane of our job when organizing kitchens. Everybody keeps too many. We had one client who had an entire pantry closet stuffed with them. Every time someone opened it—which was often—floating bags attacked! This is probably the one clutter category where the recidivism rate among some clients is terribly high. The best way to limit these bags is to give them a proper home in a plastic-bag holder, which limits how many grocery bags you can keep. When it's full, take the bags back to your grocery store. Some communities even recycle plastic bags now.

PixieTip!

Katie likes to mount a small wastebasket for holding plastic bags on the cabinet door underneath her sink. There are wastebaskets designed specifically for that purpose.

Keep a "Later Box" for stuff you can't part with now

This is one of our biggest secrets that will magically help you get rid of clutter. (Okay, maybe not *magically*. . . .) Put whatever you're trying to get rid of but can't yet part with in a box and store it away, out of sight. Revisit the box in a predetermined amount of time—usually the length it takes you to really forget about extraneous things—e.g., six months, one to two years. Before you reopen the box, list or just try to remember what's in the box. What you still can't live without is what you keep. Everything else? Donate, trash, recycle, or sell. It's okay to keep sentimental things you can't part with in storage (within reason)—*no shame, no blame!* Sometimes it takes ten-plus years for people to be able to let go of something that has a story or memory associated with it.

Kitchen

1 If your kitchen cabinets have movable shelves, use them so boxes can fit properly.

2 Avail yourself of a spice organizer (or just corral them on a lazy Susan).

3 Spaghetti and angel-hair pasta boxes usually fit perfectly when placed headfirst—not sideways.

4 Danger: Those spaghetti boxes are threatening to fall on heads!

5 Boxes at various angles are a sure sign that this cabinet needs to be decluttered and organized. Funs: get motivated right now. Classics, Organic Structures, and Smarts: put it on your To-Do list.

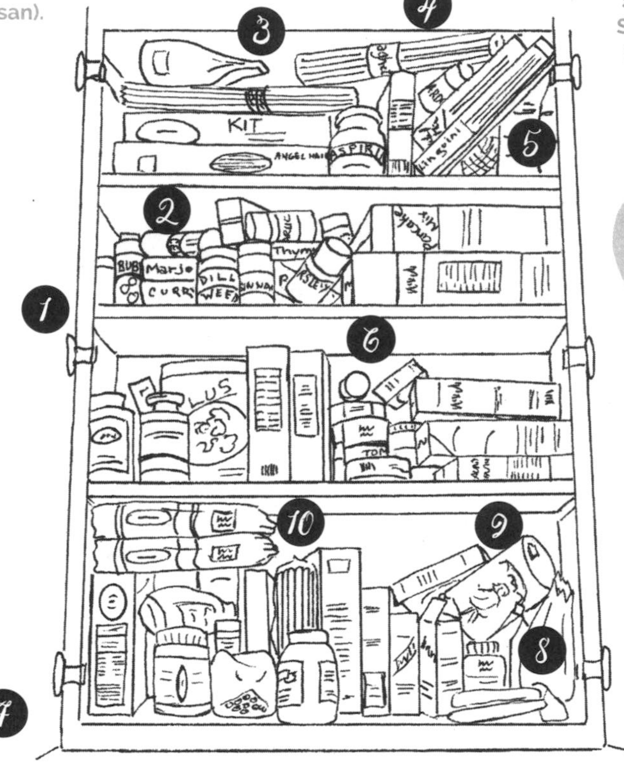

6 Lazy Susans are also a perfect solution for cans.

7 Organic Freedoms and Smart Freedoms: invite your most judgmental friend over to inspire you and help you organize.

8 Vitamins, medicines, and other small packets without structure need to be corralled in a basket or bin.

9 Canisters are perfect for . . . can you guess? Lazy Susans! You'll easily get to the stuff stashed behind.

10 Here's another sign that the shelf heights need to be rearranged. How are you supposed to get the boxes below with these on top?

1 Whatever you can't fit on lazy Susans should be ditched. This rule is a great impetus to purge for Organics and Smarts.

2 Less-used pantry items should be kept up high and on lazy Susans, so only a step stool is needed to gain access.

3 Pasta facing long-way in! Now it's easy to grab, and you're not in danger of it falling on you.

4 See? Lazy Susans are the perfect solution for cans. Save the second shelf for items you use weekly.

5 Lazy Susan to the rescue once again. Perfect for spices.

6 Voilà! The shelf is adjusted and cereal boxes fit right-side up.

7 Here's another perfectly acceptable use for a stacking shelf—it provides easy access to small items. However, stacking shelves are not for cabinets with glass doors!

CLASSIC FREEDOMS & CLASSIC STRUCTURES

Kitchen Priorities for *Classics*

- Keep countertops as sparse as possible.
- Put "purge" on your To-Do list.
- Use FIFO when you have multiples of a product in the pantry.
- Buy fridge bins.
- Get matching leftover food containers.
- Prune that bulletin board.
- Hide garbage cans.
- Acknowledge that there is more than one way to load a dishwasher.
- Classic Freedoms: limit sentimental items.
- Limit plastic grocery bags.

> *PixieTip!*
>
> Not all Classics realize that they prefer sparse surfaces until they strip a room of visual clutter and, like magic, feel more relaxed. Take a "before" photo, clear your countertops of almost everything, and then take an "after" photo. See how you feel looking at each. It's fun!

You are happiest with orderly, sparse, magazine-perfect kitchens. It's tough to maintain, but worth it. You don't like a slew of appliances on the counter, but acquiesce because storing them creates extra steps when you want to use them. This is why countertop appliance garages are a must for any kitchen update. Kitchens with open shelving or glass cabinets look amazing on Pinterest but don't translate well in your world. They're a pain in the butt to keep perfect, though you'll waste time doing it because you don't like visual clutter. Give yourself a break if you're planning a new kitchen and have at least a few cupboards with opaque doors so you can have a little hidden disarray and some things that don't match. The more structure you put in cabinets, drawers, and shelves, the more you can fit behind closed doors—and the happier you'll be. This means using *lots* of drawer bins and shelf risers. You can even get knife blocks that fit in drawers so there's one less thing on your counter.

Are you really a Classic if you haven't heard of FIFO?

Routine pruning of the pantry and dishware pays dividends toward sanity—yes, throwing out questionably stale pancake mix or a random plastic water bottle will actually help you relax. If it's not happening often, put it in your calendar until it's a habit. Harness your power to focus on details to avoid having to frequently throw out food. Check "Best By" dates when grabbing cans or boxes and use the oldest (yet still fresh) products first. Any Classic accountant or economics major—there are many of you—will recognize this as the FIFO (First In, First Out) accounting method.

Kitchens are not a place for sentimental clutter

Kitchen purging isn't simply about getting rid of food. Classic Freedoms: If you're short on space, then it's time to—heaven forbid—ditch your sentimental mugs (or their equivalents), use them elsewhere, or put them in a Later Box. Classics are happier when they have mugs that generally coordinate with dishware rather than a bunch of random ones with stories behind them. The same goes for glassware and kids' stuff, too. Regardless of space, having only matching dishware and glassware is also practical because they can be stored more uniformly and neatly.

Feed your inner organizing nerd with fridge bins and containers

You guys are the prime marketing targets for refrigerator and freezer organizing bins and containers. Buy them, and you can easily retrieve anything from your fridge—no more digging for loose items like cheese sticks and yogurts. When we first started out, it was hard to find organizing bins deep enough for conventional refrigerators, but now they are everywhere. Also, splurge on reusable glass containers for leftovers. You'll be so happy with the matching stacks of leftovers in your refrigerator; it's like buying yourself a massage, but it lasts longer. Containment gives you joy!

> *PixieTip!*
>
> You guys are the worst offenders when it comes to stashing plastic grocery bags. Invest in the reusable kind that you can fit in your purse or keep some in your car, and end the plastic invasion under your sink or—ugh—between the fridge and the counter!

Keep the bulletin board well pruned

You'll need to do more maintenance on bulletin boards than others because a messy one will annoy you. Keep it minimalistic. You're practically the only type that can keep a bulletin board sensible in appearance, yet still functional.

Hide your trash

Get a hidden wastebasket. If you don't have a built-in one, you can easily install one that pulls out under your sink or in a lower cabinet. Ditto for recycling. They're not as perfect as built-ins—which make throwing away trash just a one-step process—but you will appreciate the extra space in your kitchen. It makes rooms appear bigger.

FUN FREEDOMS & FUN STRUCTURES

Kitchen Priorities for *Funs*

- Throw things out in the moment.
- Use the local food drive as a deadline to purge.
- Fridge bins rock.
- Keep frequently used things within easy reach.
- Upgrade your kitchen stuff if you love to cook.
- Hide garbage.
- Fun Freedoms: limit sentimental items.

Inspiration and deadlines are purging's best friends

Regular pruning in your kitchen provides daily sanity, because when left to your own devices—and an "I might use this" nature—you will keep a lot of excess stale pantry and sundry items. This leads to that moment when you realize you have no idea what's in the back of your fridge. You don't need to make a big production about purging or create some routine. Instead, harness your "in the now" powers and get rid of stuff when the spirit moves you—e.g., when you are looking for curry powder and realize you have three containers of it; when those blanched almonds smell weird; or when your plastic food-container drawer no longer closes. If this piecemeal approach fails, local food drives make great deadlines to get rid of unused food that isn't past its prime. Once you're in those cupboards clearing unused food, get rid of redundant utensils, plates, and the like. Fun Freedoms: Repurpose, ditch, or store sentimental items.

Fridge bins rock!

Another way to stave off "What the heck is in the back of my fridge?" is—drumroll—fridge bins. We swear they're not overkill. You pull them out and reach what's in the back of your fridge in one step or easily corral small things like yogurts, juice boxes, and so on.

Lazy Susans and open shelves work for you

While you like orderly kitchens (many of you are cooks) and appreciate magazine-perfect kitchens, don't stress out maintaining such an impossible standard. While you don't love visual clutter, you don't mind things (e.g., olive oil, salt, pepper) being out if they're commonly used. You're a prime candidate for a lazy Susan full of cooking essentials on the countertop.

We suspect that Funs who love to cook are responsible for the trend of open kitchen shelving and hanging pot racks. Even though you like opaqueness for storage in other areas of your life, to you the kitchen is a moving organism. Your homebrew of perfectionism and utilitarianism makes you recognize that open shelving turns putting away and retrieving stuff into a one-step process. Plus, you have the patience to keep visible dishware looking decent and the wisdom to hide oddball, ugly appliances that aren't used daily.

Upgrade your kitchen stuff if it's visible and you hate it

Buy yourself coordinating quality dishware, glassware, and/or bakeware that you *want* to display, particularly if you have open shelving or are a master chef, so having everything out won't bother you. And this almost goes without saying, but we wouldn't be Pixies if we didn't remind you that when you upgrade your kitchen stuff, it means donating what you're replacing. Clutter is not encouraged!

There's no reason to stare at your trash

Hidden wastebaskets are the best. Dude, you might not be perfectly organized, but you keep a clean house. Ones custom-built into the cabinet doors are easiest, but it's not a big deal for you to install one in a lower cabinet and make the effort of opening the door to pull it out.

ORGANIC STRUCTURES & SMART STRUCTURES

Kitchen Priorities for *Organic/Smart Structures*

- Minimize countertop clutter.
- Do a big purge, and then pare down annually.
- Buy matching leftover food containers.
- Any trash can works for you.
- Have a junk drawer.
- Organic Structures: limit sentimental items.

Dude, limit what's out on your countertop

You keep orderly kitchens, and while you don't need barren countertops to love your kitchen, things can get unruly there (not to mention inside your fridge and cabinets). Make sure you regularly use what's on the counter. There's efficiency to having things out . . . and then there's not having enough counter space to cook. We know one Organic Structure who keeps her Nespresso® pods out by her machine for easy morning coffee—those sorts of things should be out. If you're redoing a kitchen, don't bother with glass doors or open shelving—they're a nightmare to keep looking nice—but *do* consider building an appliance garage. Otherwise, keep infrequently used appliances out of sight. When you install pullout shelves on lower cabinets, it makes retrieving these appliances easier.

Schedule a purge

If your cupboard, drawers, and fridge are stuffed and you can't easily find kitchen gadgets, pantry items, or condiments, then it's time to schedule a purge. Oddly, you do better purging when you start organizing *first*, so set to work on your cooking-utensil drawer. Large drawer organizers are useful but not necessary; it's better for you to have the tools you use frequently out on the countertop in *one* cylinder. If you have more than one, the utensils will quickly overtake your counter space faster than breeding rabbits. We had an Organic

Structure client with *three* cylinders out—there are three-star Michelin chefs that don't use that many cooking utensils in a week. Going forward, prune everything (pantry, dishware, flatware, etc.) at least annually—put it on your calendar as a recurring event. It'll take you two seconds if you discard things that are smelly, duplicates, or semi-broken. Organic Structures: put unused sentimental items that you refuse to part with in a Later Box.

PixieTip!

We'll never understand using contact paper in cabinets if you've thoroughly cleaned the shelves, but cushiony contact paper on shelves housing fragile items can be great for Organics and Smarts who break a lot of glassware.

When lacking space to devote an entire drawer to junk, a bowl on the countertop can act as a substitute.

You don't have to hold on to every food container that crosses your path

You're not the most likely to buy a slew of matching leftover food containers, because you probably have a hodgepodge of existing bins that are stuffed in the fridge helter-skelter. We also know that persuading you to buy new things to replace perfectly good items is often a losing battle. With that said, we will just add that you'll find things in your fridge much more easily when there's order to your leftover containers. Also, consider using a lazy Susan in your fridge if you have lots of condiments that overflow into the fridge from your fridge-door bins.

Any old wastebasket will do

As for wastebaskets, you guys can handle any kind and size—hidden or sitting out, because you'll reliably take out the trash and don't mind the extra visual clutter. But fight your practical nature and get one that you don't hate looking at with a foot pedal for easier access.

Whoever invented junk drawers is a genius

Junk drawers are not a sign of failure; they're an unconventional, formalized place to corral miscellany that have no obvious home but don't belong in the trash yet. They keep clutter at bay on countertops, freeing them up for things like cooking. But purge annually: if it hasn't been needed in a year, chances are it no longer needs to be in your home.

ORGANIC FREEDOMS & SMART FREEDOMS

Kitchen Priorities for Organic/Smart Freedoms

- More lazy Susans, please!
- Keep things visible.
- Minimize countertop clutter.
- Use deadlines to purge.
- Chain a pen to your grocery list.
- Big trash cans out in the open, or behind a door, are best.
- Have at least one junk drawer.
- Organic Freedoms limit sentimental items

Your home may not be the societal ideal of organizing perfection, but you, too, would like to find the ketchup or the cheese grater! Your best bet to keeping things organized in here is to make things easy (i.e., as close to one step as possible) to put away and retrieve. Anything that can reasonably fit on a lazy Susan should go on one—even in the fridge. What storage space you lose in having so many, you gain in easily finding what's there. By contrast, if, at some point in your life, you admire some Classic's matching cylinders of dry goods and try it yourself, you will deeply regret it every time you buy a box of cereal.

PixieTip!

Wall-mounted knife magnets or knife blocks without specific slots are easier for you than a knife block where you have to figure out what specific slot to put each knife in.

If you see it, you'll know where it is

Think pot racks and open shelving. They make retrieving and storing kitchen stuff into a one-step process—no pesky cabinet doors serving as an extra step when putting things away. You'll find your cheese grater because it is right in front of your eyes. Before you call us crazy and protest that it'll be a mess, let us reassure you that you can keep open shelves *appearing* tidy as long as things match—e.g., similar glasses, plates that coordinate, nice pots and pans. You might wonder why we suggest matching since this aesthetic isn't as important to you as it is to others; but when you have items that coordinate, they still look deliberate and organized, no matter how they are strewn about on the shelves. A strong word of caution: trouble starts if you add bits and bobs that don't match, or you start putting pantry items out on the shelves, which is why everyone needs a few closed, opaque cabinet doors in their kitchen.

> **Pixie Tip!**
>
> Be wary of glass cabinet doors. You'll be attracted to them, but why go through all the trouble of getting matching everything and then *not* eliminate the extra step of opening a cupboard door when retrieving and putting items away?

Countertops are not junk drawers

Chances are you're going to have cluttered countertops, and it will not bug you enough to do anything about it—unless you're living with a different personality type. Limit what's out on the counter to items and appliances you use most frequently (there's no reason coffee can't sit out next to the coffee maker, for example). If you don't want to forget the existence of things you don't use frequently—e.g., a mixer or a panini grill—leave them out. Most of you will make it look aesthetically nice. The only caveat is to ensure that you have adequate countertop space left to prep and cook.

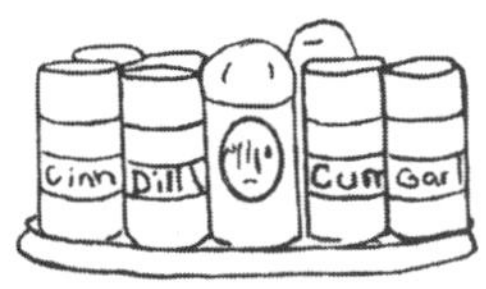

Use deadlines to purge

Try to declutter this room once a year—ahead of a big party, the holidays, or a local food drive so it'll get done. If that fails, do it when you're motivated (e.g., "Argh! Where is the freaking ketchup?"). Just make sure you've got a clear schedule; otherwise you might only get a quarter of the way through tearing up your kitchen before you remember you've got to be somewhere—leaving the kitchen quite disorganized, potentially for a long, long time. To avoid these disastrous situations, another option is to tackle discrete projects, such as throwing out old food and condiments in the fridge, instead of the whole shebang all at once.

Pre-make your grocery list

If you decide to keep a running grocery list, try to place a dedicated pen next to the pad. If there was a way to chain it to the pad, we'd tell you to do it! But in the real world, buy a pencil with a magnet attached.

PixieTip!

Eliminate decision-making whenever possible. For example, a perfect utensil solution for a Smart Freedom client incapable of putting silverware in the right utensil bin might be a bin with cutout shapes of the cutlery, which offers limited room for errors or decisions.

Whiteboards with a pen holder can also work as lists if you photograph them before leaving, but not if someone forgets to put the special pen back in its holder.

Fight your urge to hide trash

Step-top cans out in the open are the best solution for you. It's aesthetically nice to have hidden trash cans, especially if you have a custom built-in one. But if you don't? Avoid installing a pullout one, as opening a cupboard door and then pulling out trash are too many steps for some of you to do every time you want to throw something out. Make sure you don't have a lid on a wastebasket that's inside a cupboard or under a sink—too many steps. Go big if you've got the room, so you don't have to take the trash out too often.

You guys invented junk drawers

Finally, having a junk drawer or two isn't a sign of organizational failure; it's a designated place to put things in the "What in the heck is this? Is it important?" category. Proudly wear this unconventional solution on your sleeve. The next time you purge, just make sure to go through them and get rid of anything you can't identify or haven't used in two years. If you've got three junk drawers in the kitchen, Kelly would argue that perhaps you never purged this room or created proper homes for things . . . but Katie wears her three-junk-drawer badge with pride.

Sentimental items are for décor or use

Organic Freedoms might be attached to things in their kitchen, and there's nothing wrong with that—as long as they're used in the kitchen or are part of the décor (i.e., "aesthetically useful"). If not, ditch them or put them in a Later Box.

Kitchen Checklist

- ☐ Purged your kitchen of expired food and spices, as well as excess pot lids, sentimental mugs, and other useless items
- ☐ Tossed or donated duplicates, dull knives, and mismatched plastic food containers
- ☐ Moved rarely used items to another space to save room (if applicable)
- ☐ Measured the entire kitchen and returned any (unopened) unused or ill-fitting organizational products to the store
- ☐ Organized cupboards by storing like with like and making sure the flatware, dishware, cups, and glasses are within easy reach of the dishwasher
- ☐ Installed pullout drawers (lower cabinets) and shelf risers (upper cabinets) to maximize space and make retrieval easier
- ☐ Bought organizers, bins, and lazy Susans for corralling spices, cutlery, and other narrow items used daily
- ☐ Purchased organizers for pot lids as well as cutting boards and baking pans
- ☐ Installed a bulletin board for things like invitations and kids' artwork that often go on the refrigerator door
- ☐ Placed a notepad and pen on or near the refrigerator for jotting down grocery needs
- ☐ Corralled kitchen cleaning supplies in a transportable caddy under the sink
- ☐ Bought a plastic-bag holder or extra wastebasket and got rid of excess plastic bags that don't fit in them
- ☐ Started using the magical "Later Box" for clutter you can't part with

CHAPTER EIGHT

The Dining Room

If you've got junk, papers, and coats strewn around this room, it's because you haven't set up an *appropriate* place to go through your mail, a proper home-office area in which to store it, and somewhere easy to hang up your coats, purses, backpacks, sports gear, and so on. Without these systems in place, the dining-room table—with its irresistible clean surface—will quickly become the depository of what we like to call "inappropriate" storage. The easiest way to avoid this is the golden dining rule: "Thou shalt not use your dining room as a home office." If you can do this, then the dining room will be the easiest room to organize, as the solutions are almost *all* universal—except for a few caveats for different types.

UNIVERSAL SOLUTIONS

Dining-Room Essentials for *All Types*

- Organize entryway and home office first.
- Don't make it a multipurpose room.
- Get a table and chairs that fit so people can easily get in and out.
- Only store items used in this room.
- Have adequate storage for china, tablecloths, place mats, etc.
- Install a dimmer switch for magical dining experiences.

Dining rooms are for *dining*

Some of you can work in here—as long as it's easy for you to leave no trace behind. It's one of those *know and accept who you are* moments. Nobody wants to dine where a computer sits or tax forms linger. We don't know exactly why, but if a dining table doubles as anything, it immediately stops being used for dining. Ditto for a kitchen table. We know there are people reading this, thinking, "Well, I have a desk in my dining area, and we dine in there," but trust us: the room would be a lot more inviting for meals without a desk or papers hanging out.

Find furniture that fits

Regardless of who you are, you need the basic furniture: a table, chairs, and a console and/or a tall hutch. Outside of using your dining area as a home office or entry table, nothing kills a dining area quicker than having trouble accessing all of the chairs or cupboards. Hand-me-down tables are great, but if they don't fit, get something that does. It's worth the extra trouble—trust us. Everyone

> **PixieTip!**
>
> If you're short on space, acrylic ghost dining chairs give the illusion of more space and literally blend into the woodwork!

Pixie Tip!

Have any broken china? If you're a Fun, Organic Freedom, or Smart Freedom, fix it or ditch it when you organize this room. If you're a Classic, Organic Structure, or Smart Structure, fix it or ditch it while organizing the room—or add the task to your To-Do list. Otherwise, you'll be storing useless broken china for no reason.

Yes, you can put sterling silver in the dishwasher, as long as it's separated from stainless steel; otherwise it'll tarnish. Ditto for nice china. Sure, gold or silver plate will wear down over time in a dishwasher, but it'll take a lifetime to wear off completely.

should have a relaxing place to break bread that isn't a kitchen island or a TV tray.

Get adequate storage—for dining accoutrements only

Make sure you have enough storage for whatever dining and entertaining accoutrements you have, be they candlesticks, silverware, tablecloths, place-mats, serving platters, china, napkins, or other items. Many personality types put random items in the "good china" cupboard. Avoid this. The more clutter you hide away in there, the harder it will be to use the stuff you actually need to dine *easily*. If you've got things in here that don't get used in the dining room, find them new homes around the house or give them away.

Ambiance matters

Take the time and expense to install dimmers for the lights in here, so you don't kill every meal with bright light. It's much easier to do than you might think; it's not expensive to have an electrician do it for you, either. We swear you'll wonder why you didn't install the dimmer switch the minute you moved in, and it is probably the real reason you don't eat dinner as a family anymore! Another ambiance booster is table décor. It's not that expensive to buy silver-plated silverware on eBay® or www.replacements.com, and silver elevates a table setting. (*Downton Abbey* wasn't a massive hit *just* because of the juicy plot.)

CLASSIC STRUCTURES & CLASSIC FREEDOMS

Dining-Room Priorities for Classics

- Be formal.
- Have appropriate storage for nice things and a few hiding places for clutter.
- It's okay to have plastic covers for your good dining chairs.

You are a Classic: own it

Classics *invented* formal dining rooms. As practical as you are, it will bug you to have to share your dining area with anything other than a beautiful china cabinet, table, and matching chairs. Sure, some of you may grow used to a dual-use dining room, and even if lack of space forces you to eat off of a TV table, it's still technically a table—you're not the type to eat straight out of a giant bag of chips on your sofa. Short on dining space in a condo or apartment? Get a drop-leaf table in your living area to demarcate a dining area. You can pull it out to create a quick, elegant dining surface, and it takes up less space than a regular table when not in use.

If space has forced you to have a "TV-tray-table dining room," be sure to get a unit that stores those tables away when not in use.

Get appropriate storage, with some hiding spaces

Have some storage space hidden behind cupboard doors, so all your storage doesn't have to be perfect-looking. There are more important things in life than making sure your cabinet looks good at all times. If you've got a lot of china plates stacked on each other, you can use cabinet risers to create more space. If you have silver or silver-plate flatware, make sure to get a chest for it, as it'll protect it from tarnishing, and you'll have no problem keeping it organized. If you have more than twelve settings, get two chests. Multiple drawers in a cabinet are also a great way for you to separate by function: napkins and napkin holders in one; place mats in the other.

Dining Room

1 A dining room hutch is the perfect place for office supplies. . . . Wait, *no*!

2 Here's more stuff that shouldn't be on a dining-room table. Perhaps the home office or entryway.

3 This window is wearing no clothes!

4 Decorating 101: nothing goes on top of a bookshelf or hutch.

5 Um, a chair is not an appropriate home for a printer.

6 A laptop is okay if you're a Classic or a Fun, but the printer, office supplies, and piles on the table are signs that an Organic or Smart has taken up residence.

7 Kids' shoes especially need homes . . . along with a tyrannical grown-up to make sure their owners get into the habit of putting shoes away.

8 Boots and a backpack? Time to check the entryway and see if there's a home for these items

9 Who wants to eat in a dog kennel?

1 There's room for a centerpiece. Yay!

2 China in a china cupboard? Madness. . . . It looks good, right?

3 The windows are properly attired, which draws the eye up and makes the room seem taller.

4 Without the large objects on top we can breathe easy that nothing's going to fall down on us during dinner.

5 Dining-room dimmer switches are essential for ambiance. Bonus: you don't run the risk of burning your house down with candles.

6 Now there's an extra chair within reach for guests.

7 The inappropriate dog kennel has left the dining room, as it should.

8 Repeat after us: "A dining room table is for *dining* items"

If you can, Sunbrella® instead of plastic

As for plastic covers for dining chairs, you guys are the type most likely to buy them, and, if you must—you've got kids or particularly messy Organic or Smart relatives—just remember to take them off for "good" company. (Yes, Classic Kelly keeps them on for her children, parents, and siblings!) But a warning: nothing says "I'm secretly (or openly) a cranky old lady or gentleman" like plastic covers on furniture. In addition, it's annoying and an extra step to take them on and off, so they usually stay on the chairs. Better yet, keep judgment at bay by upholstering dining chairs with Sunbrella® indoor/outdoor fabric. It comes in a million patterns and is designed to be cleaned easily.

FUN STRUCTURES & FUN FREEDOMS

Dining-Room Priorities for *Funs*

- Get a "Great Room."
- Mix and match, but don't go overboard.
- Open shelves are fine.
- No desks allowed in your formal dining room.

We're pretty sure you invented the "Great Room"

We suspect you're responsible for replacing distinct family rooms and kitchen nooks with the ubiquitous "Great Room"—and by that, we mean the big open space that combines kitchen, dining room, and living room. These "rooms" make sense as a gathering space for eating, working, reposing, and laughing, since people tend to gather and hang in the kitchen anyway. And you won't have to disappear into the kitchen when having convivial parties! Create a Great Room for yourself if you don't have one already. The reason? If most of your life is all inside one big room, it allows you to effortlessly get things done the moment you think about it and have the time.

You're a Fun: own it (but don't go crazy)

Even if you *do* have a separate formal dining room, you don't have to get all the traditional furniture, like a console and hutch. You could have a piano or books on bookshelves in here, and this "mixed" aesthetic probably wouldn't bug you, nor create too much clutter. You're flexible if the situation warrants it. Of course, you can use whatever cupboard floats your boat—solid cabinet doors, glass-enclosed, or open-shelf—but if it's not your inclination to go with formal, then don't. The one nod to conventionality you should consider? Flatware chests. It'll save you the hassle of cleaning the silver frequently, and you'll put things back in their appropriate slots.

Open shelving is A-OK

You don't have to hide stuff away behind cupboards in here, because either messy china will not bug you or, if it does, you'll take the time to make it look nice. Open shelves, whether mounted or bookshelves, can double as storage. Just remember to get low, flat bins that fit on these shelves to store napkins, place mats, and the like. They're hard to keep tidy on open shelves.

Desks are a no-no

No, we're not backing up the truck and green-lighting a home office in a formal dining room. Ignore us all you want, but you know we're right about this one.

ORGANIC STRUCTURES, ORGANIC FREEDOMS, SMART STRUCTURES, & SMART FREEDOMS

Dining-Room Priorities for Organics and Smarts

- A formal dining room means you can keep it neat and be messy elsewhere.
- Open storage in here works.
- You can have silverware boxes, but Ziploc bags are so much easier.

Leave messes for the kitchen and living areas

Yes, this chapter is so simple that we can lump all Organics and Smarts together. We know you appreciate and want a "Great Room" of your own if you don't already have one. But the benefit of a formal, separate dining room is that it's easier to keep an eating-only room neat if you've got other spaces to cook in, live in, and get a little messy. Make sure you have a home office somewhere else, though.

This is the only place Smarts can have glass cabinets

The dining room is the one place in which glass cabinet doors are not an idiotic obstacle for Smarts, *as long as* you only store the good china in there and don't use it every day. Seeing it will remind you of its existence. While in theory this should also hold true for Organics, you tend to have a lot of sentimental china that doesn't jibe with the neat stacks of teacups and good china, so you'll also need to mix in closed storage. Before hiding mismatched sentimental stuff away, make sure you're likely to use everything in there. If not, put it into a Later Box, donate, or sell. Smarts will likely throw the broken china away, sentimental or not. Organic Structures: revisit it in a couple of years to see if you can get rid of more. Organic Freedoms: revisit this stuff when you're in that mode again or you feel like your attic is about to fall in on you. And those doing open shelving: remember to get low, flat bins that fit on these shelves to store napkins, place mats, and other items—or find a drawer in the kitchen for them.

Zippered baggies are a lifesaver

We thought we'd found every use for these plastic baggies—wet bathing suits, soiled baby clothes, travel bags for kids' toys, etc.—but we've just uncovered an additional use: storing silver flatware. If you never take the time to put each piece of silverware in its proper slot—like our Organic Structure client whose silver chest looked as if she didn't realize there were slots—then forego the silver flatware chest altogether. They're an unnecessary step when Ziploc bags do such a bang-up job of keeping silver untarnished, and they can easily go in drawers or lie flat behind opaque cabinet doors.

Dining-Room Checklist

- ☐ Got rid of your dining-room home office and any double-duty stuff in this room
- ☐ Replaced ill-fitting furniture
- ☐ Found new homes for items not used in the dining room
- ☐ Purchased adequate, appropriate dining-room furniture and storage
- ☐ Installed dimmer switch, and you're enjoying mood lighting over dinner forever . . .

CHAPTER NINE

The Family and Living Rooms

The main problem we encounter with these rooms is inefficient furniture layouts and designs. We've found that educating our clients about a few basic design rules helps these rooms function better—no matter what's gone wrong. Whether or not you have the money to buy new décor, we highly recommend the book *Use What You Have® Decorating* by Lauri Ward, which teaches the decorating basics beyond what we've included in this chapter. You'll be amazed by what all the basic design rules do for your home and its organization.

UNIVERSAL SOLUTIONS

Family- and Living-Room Essentials for *All Types*

- Limit how many purposes these rooms serve.
- Ensure that multipurposes are separate and conducive to each other.
- Create a classic U-shaped conversation pit.
- Your TV doesn't have to be a focal point.
- Have enough storage and tables.
- Declutter and digitize.
- Create a wall photo gallery.
- Hide toys.
- Only hardcover books belong in these rooms.

Limit multipurposes

Living areas are often multipurpose rooms—TV room, kids' playroom, and/or home office—and in serving many masters they can easily accumulate unnecessary clutter, which is a bummer since they're also the place where guests spend the most time. How to keep clutter to a minimum? Minimize multipurposes. If this isn't possible, then make sure the multipurposes are distinct yet conducive to each other—i.e., put a home office in a corner that isn't part of the main seating area, and make sure it matches the décor. A work desk should only hold office stuff, not DVDs or a game console. Office supplies and toys need proper, permanent, hidden homes so that you can completely close up the office or playroom when it's time to be an adult or entertain. Think: armoire desk with a hidden shelf or drawer for

PixieTip!

Remember the formal living room that was essentially roped off to anyone but the best guests? It turns out your grandparents were on to something. We know one young Classic who doesn't allow her children to spend time there unless they're entertaining. No children = less mess.

a printer, dedicated toy shelves with multiple opaque toy bins behind a couch, coordinating fabric panels that hide office and toy paraphernalia. Sipping a drink next to a printer the size of Gibraltar would be off-putting to anyone.

Your furniture layout sucks

Outside of clutter, the biggest complaint we hear about living areas is that nobody hangs out or interacts in them. The solution is usually as quick as rearranging your existing furniture so the layout is conducive to both conversation and relaxation. For this to happen, you need a U-shaped conversation pit around the couch (e.g., a couch with two chairs opposite it or off to the side). Adhering to proper furniture layouts like this helps rooms function better. It's one of the first lessons in Lauri Ward's book for a reason. We implemented this idea for a client who had a hair studio just off her living room. Within minutes of placing two dining chairs opposite her couch, the three men waiting in silence to get their haircuts started jabbering away like old friends. This taught us that it's not as much about the comfort of the chairs opposite the couch as it is about the U-formation. Avoid an L-shape—a couch with one chair or a chaise sectional—but if this is your setup, get at least one occasional chair or stool to turn the "L" into a "U." Someone will use it—we promise!

> **PixieTip!**
>
> Furniture pushed up against walls is a conversation-killer but impossible to do once you implement a true U-shape formation.

Also, one of the most common mistakes people make in this room is having seating too far away from their coffee table: Eighteen inches (46 cm) is the best distance. The best sofa seat height is around sixteen or seventeen inches (40–43 cm), and the coffee table should be roughly the same height.

TVs are eyesores

As for your televisions, don't hate us, but they really shouldn't be blocking windows. Make sure they are roughly at eye level when you're seated—it's hard to relax and watch the boob tube when you're craning your neck. If you've only got one living area, the TV shouldn't be the center of attention. Search "Hide TV" on Pinterest to find clever places and ways to hide a television. The best solution is to build a whole unit around the television so it's not one lonely, massive, ugly centerpiece. A cheaper option is "minimizing" a television by surrounding it with pictures. The television eyesore then becomes one picture among many in a gallery! Or you can paint the TV wall dark. Worst case: hang it over the fireplace with a special mount, and keep the cable box and modem in a media cabinet nearby. But if you're hanging it, make sure it's situated roughly six to eight inches (15–20 cm) above a piece of furniture (ditto for paintings).

Everybody has extra, unused wires and items in their TV area. Sometimes it's a comical tangled mess. At a minimum, make sure these ugly items are behind cabinet doors or in a bin.

> *PixieTip!*
>
> The first thing you want to see when walking into a room, besides a focal point like a fireplace, is the sofa—to invite guests and yourself to sit down, take a load off, and relax.

Have adequate storage and surface space

Everyone needs a media console to store unsightly cords, video games, cable boxes, and so on—and not some horrid metal-and-glass contraption that shows off a fancy amplifier and receiver and surround-sound speakers. Your television console—especially if it's in your only formal living room—should be a nice piece of furniture at least as big as your television, with hidden space for utilitarian electronics. Infrared devices enable you to hide these without rendering them useless or hard to reach. Your best bet is to buy a media console that surrounds the television with shelving and cabinet storage to draw attention away from the eyesore. Plus, you get the bonus of extra storage—always wise—to accommodate all the random bits and bobs that sneak into this room.

Having matching lamps and side tables on either side of the couch improves the functionality of these rooms. We also find that many clients don't have large enough coffee tables or ottomans, with trays substituting as such. To figure out if they're big enough, imagine being a guest in your own home.

Sit down in all the available seats and ask yourself where you would put down your glass. Can you reach the nearest surface without having to stand up?

Ditch clutter you don't love

Oh, and then there are all those tchotchkes, picture frames, magazines, catalogs, DVDs, and so on. Make sure you *love* all your random things and that they fit with the living room's décor. Magazines should be current, few, and stored in a separate container. The same goes for catalogs.

Digitize

Digitize your music and DVD library so you have your favorite tunes, movies, and TV shows stored in the cloud and not your living area. Either do the project yourself over time, or hire someone to do it for you. As a bonus, it allows you to watch movies on multiple devices—not just the TV with the disc player.

Speaking of digitizing, many people keep family albums in their living areas. If you have shoe boxes full of old photos, it's easier to play catch-up on making albums when photos are digitized. You can digitize photos using a bulk mail service or, if you're concerned about the safety of your collection, there are organizers you can hire who specialize in organizing photos and making albums *for* you. No joke. In the words of our favorite photo organizer, Isabelle Dervaux, "Enjoy your photographs—don't stash them away."

Create a wall photo gallery

Another common problem in living and family rooms is the ever-present hodgepodge of photo frames. Slowly but surely, people give them to you, and then before you know it your side tables, bookshelves, and mantel are all covered. Clear frames off utilized surfaces, like side tables and bookshelves, and find spots for them that are not blocking the utility of furniture. The best way to do this is to create photo-gallery walls with matching or coordinating matted frames in your underutilized hallways or staircases. You can get great affordable pre-matted frames from Pottery Barn or West Elm® that often come with templates and design suggestions for how to arrange them.

Hide the toys

If, God forbid, you have to share your living area with toys, then think about positioning your couch so that the toy storage is hidden behind it. Couch tables with cabinets and shelves are perfect storage vehicles for toys in multipurpose living areas.

PixieTip!

Make your living room look like it was designed by a professional by ensuring your artwork isn't too small for the room and that it's anchored to a piece of furniture either below or at eye level.

Books happen—here's how to deal

Even with the advent of e-books and the cloud, and while we find fewer and fewer DVD and photo-album collections in the course of our work with clients, every type seems to hang on to their books (even textbooks), especially if you've merged your household with someone else's or were raised by a bibliophile.

To reduce clutter on living-room bookshelves, we suggest a hardcover-only rule in here. Consider keeping paperbacks in the family room or bedroom, where there are not as many prying eyes. Paperbacks are meant to be recycled unless they are truly out of print or still read. Donate hardcovers you don't care about anymore. Let that poor neglected book be loved by someone, man! Keep only books that have meaning, that you read, that make you happy, or that frankly look good in a display. Once you take these steps, your books become more like objets d'art than utilitarian fountains of knowledge.

Avoid placing photos and tchotchkes *in front of* books, as it makes retrieving them into a three-step process, but if you're lacking space and keep the books more for décor than reading, it's okay. If you want bookshelves to look even less cluttered, let go of the dust jackets. You can still organize books by subject. To take it a step further, organize books by color and size within their subject matter and break up the long lines of vertically stacked books with a horizontal stack here and there and/or a few photographs. You can sometimes even get away with putting a photo or tchotchke on top of a small pile of horizontally stacked books. Your guests will be impressed the next time they see this artful display of books interspersed with your choicest tchotchkes and photographs.

Living Room

1 This artwork is a good size for the room, but it's hung too high.

2 The windows are like, "Hello, I'm naked."

3 Is this an office, a living room, or a playroom?

4 While a hutch like this is essential for Organics and Smarts, it's just too much clutter for a living room.

5 Mismatched frames make cluttered and messy what could look nice.

6 Open shelving for cable boxes and stereo equipment makes the room look even more cluttered.

7 This coffee table has too much mess with mismatched photos, games, and random toys underneath. Time to organize!

8 There's not enough storage for the toys, which makes the room look more chaotic than it is (and impossible to clean at the end of the day).

9 Where's the chair? Only two people can have a conversation in here.

10 Pretend you're a guest in your own home. Now: where can you set a glass down?

1 This artwork is a good size for the room, anchored to the sofa, and large enough to compete with the TV for the center of attention.

2 If windows are the eyes, then curtains are the eyebrows. The room looks a bit funny without them.

3 A chandelier (sized depending on ceiling height) is great for an instantly decorative look—even in a rental. And you can take it with you when you move.

4 Here's a desk chair that matches the décor and also doubles as an extra seat.

5 A hutch above the desk is too much clutter for this room. However, it's necessary for Organics and Smarts, which is why home offices don't belong in the living room.

6 Frames are matching and facing forward, bringing cohesion to the collection and attention away from the massive TV.

7 Attractive mesh-covered cabinet doors are perfect. Glass also works, but infrared gadgets can get around wood doors, too.

8 This coffee table, which uses a shelf below for magazines, can actually hold a coffee cup and clearly house the remote.

9 Yes! Here, a matching chair completes the classic U formation, which works for all types. Now you can talk and watch TV.

10 Where are the toys? Hidden behind the chair, perhaps?

11 Finally—a place to set down a drink!

CLASSIC FREEDOMS & CLASSIC STRUCTURES

Family- and Living-Room Essentials for *Classics*

- Don't have a multipurpose living room.
- Hide clutter related to multipurposes (because the above directive is almost impossible).
- Matching is soothing.
- Get professional help.

Keep it simple

You're happiest if the living room is not multipurpose. If you have the space, go with your traditional sensibilities and maintain both a formal living room and a family room. Having these rooms separate will also give you more space to display tchotchkes, collections, and photographs without their appearing cluttered.

Hidden is always better

Now, if you're stuck with a multipurpose living room, we're sorry, but your knack for maintaining organization will make it easier for you to keep a multipurpose room tidier than other types *once* you have proper homes for everything. What we often find when we organize a Classic's multipurpose living areas is that the organization has been put in place quickly to solve a problem, much like putting a pot underneath a ceiling drip. It's ad hoc and not well-thought-out, with mismatched containers everywhere.

When you're setting up this room, the key is to push your preferences and think longterm (not simply "How can I corral these annoying toys today?"). Create enough hidden homes for all the things that must be stored in here. Think floor-to-ceiling bookcase and cabinets with opaque doors. They don't have to be built in; they just have to be tall, coordinated, and with cabinets at the bottom to hide riffraff like office stuff, wires, or toys. Get matching opaque baskets for shelves if the cabinets are not sufficient to store items you don't want to see.

Matching is soothing

When it comes to décor, you guys were the ones who created furniture sets, which is understandable since they're efficient and practical—two things in which you excel. A room is furnished after one purchase—yes, please! But we're not suggesting you buy furniture sets; just make sure the décor is seamless and matching. Don't apologize for your traditional tastes; matching components are soothing to you, and that's the point of this relaxation room, *n'est-ce pas*?

> *PixieTip!*
>
> Classic Freedoms: do your best to curate any beloved tchotchkes and photo frames. Remember: the less clutter that's out, the more you'll enjoy this room.

In a dream world, invest in a decorator who can take your décor to the next level and do magical things like coordinate matching yet contrasting fabric and respect your tastes. Or just borrow someone else's grand vision by mimicking something you love in Pinterest or a magazine. We only suggest this because we suspect that some of you stick with traditional because design can be daunting. We guarantee: if you go the extra mile in this room, it will make your heart sing every time you enter.

FUN FREEDOMS & FUN STRUCTURES

Family- and Living-Room Essentials for Funs

- Hide clutter related to multipurposes.
- Develop a grand plan for this room.
- Break some rules.

Hide clutter on the fly

You can handle multipurpose rooms because you're not rigid about things. Even still, delineate separate spaces for each purpose of the room. Keep separate, hidden homes for ugly things so nothing sitting out annoys you. You should love your living space as much as something you covet in a celluloid image.

Décor-wise, you're good at the art of coordinating, mixing, and (not) matching things, as well as finding inventive ways to hide clutter with things you have sitting around—closed baskets, vintage luggage, pretty bins, and the like. Keep clutter at bay by using your instinct to get things done in the moment and purge stuff whenever you notice it. Less clutter = more relaxation. Before you know it, the mess is contained—practical, beautiful, done.

Go big or go home

One danger with organizing on the fly is that when you hide clutter in pre-existing bins, it keeps adding up and up, to the point where your tiny solutions are all over your living area, as if a groundhog was digging up piles and putting them in boxes. Sure, the piles are coordinated and contained, but one can only artfully place so many vintage hatboxes around a living area before being one step away from starring in a hoarding show.

Step outside your comfort zone and think big—a large bookshelf, credenza, storage desk, or cabinet/shelving unit. Then keep a few of your coordinating storage bins and baskets to serve as decorative addendums. Doing so will create a room that looks grander while giving it a more serene feel. Outside of the practicality of providing a hangout space, serenity is what these rooms should provide.

Know when and when *not to* break the rules

Some of you are naturally gifted at décor. Assuming this is you, then break a ton of décor rules when it comes to things like fabrics and matching items. *But* when it comes to basics like furniture placement, distance between furniture, wall photo galleries, or having a reachable spot to place your drink without getting up? Follow the rules.

ORGANIC STRUCTURES & SMART STRUCTURES

Family- and Living-Room Essentials for Organic/Smart Structures

- Go big with storage to contain your collections.
- Curate collections.
- Mix hidden and open storage.

Tchotchkes, books, and photos—*oh, my!*

You are instinctive grand planners who know how to make living-area décor look good. While photographs, books, and tchotchkes appear in the living areas of all types, man oh man do you guys take it to the next level. Usually, Smart Structures have a ton of books, and Organic Structures have a ridiculous amount of sentimental tchotchkes and photographs, so when it comes to setting up the storage bones for this room, you'd both better go big—floor-to-ceiling bookshelves!

Curate collections

Your living-area troubles are often related to your collections—either their arrangement or lack of curating. We don't mean getting rid of things *necessarily* (breathe!); we mean categorizing them to give more visible coherence. Other folks collect ceramic pitchers in shades of a hue for no other reason than that it goes with their décor. Not you. Whatever you display has a story behind it, reflecting you and your life. Smart Structures: you are visual "big picture" thinkers who see your books, plaques, photographs, and collectibles as a visual display of your accomplishments, interests, and goals. Organic Structures: you also surround yourselves with visual reminders of your life—objets d'art from your travels, photographs of loved ones, books that feel like friends—which is fundamentally why you guys don't part with this sort of "clutter" as easily as others and why many of your collections don't match, thus making it difficult to organize them.

We have two client Organic Structure/Smart Structure couples—one in the city, one in the burbs—but neither has a room in their homes without a floor-to-ceiling bookshelf or two (yes, including the dining rooms . . .). What's great was that they used all the vertical space in their homes to properly organize and store their precious books—but, boy, did they need to declutter! Organic Structures: have your most judgmental, ruthless Classic friend come over and make you justify every tchotchke. Smart Structures: do the same, or hire an organizer to make you justify the logic of holding on to paperbacks you can get online. All of you should channel your inner Mari Kondo and make sure everything and every book that surrounds you evokes joy. Failing that, at least buy matching frames for your photos, so at least *that* part of your collection has cohesion. Your purge is done when you have extra space for more books instead of stacks of books on your floor.

PixieTip!

Get rid of paperbacks that are attainable electronically or falling apart. If you can get an e-book version, you'll create room for more books . . . which are inevitable.

Mix hidden and visible storage

You likely have piles—magazines, catalogs, etc.—in this room, even if it's not a multipurpose living area with a home office. They should be visible if you want to actually go through them. You'll forget about them behind cabinet doors, so get open, transparent bins to give piles more structure and purpose when they're visible. Piles without bins always get messy at some point. It's especially important to do this if you live with someone who is more detail-oriented. As for storing other items, try to keep it open, but if what's sitting out detracts from the décor—e.g., a Dora the Explorer playhouse or your ugly printer—then you also need hidden storage (cabinet doors).

ORGANIC FREEDOMS & SMART FREEDOMS

Family- and Living-Room Essentials for *Organic/Smart Freedoms*

- Multipurpose living areas are a bad idea.
- Go big with storage to contain your collections.
- Ditch the low-hanging fruit as you reorganize your tableaus.
- Open storage is your best bet.

We have a bad feeling about this . . .

It's almost essential that you have separate living and family rooms if you have kids, no playroom, and you're in charge of keeping things tidy. If not, then do your best, but it's going to be endless chaos until the kids are grown and take their toys with them. As the most Zen of types, you might be able to realize that this too shall pass—and acquiesce to all the clutter, toys, and stuff that doesn't belong in a formal living room. But for your sanity, tuck away a few toys here in attractive bins, or invest in vintage toys that match your décor so the kids can play by your side while you entertain.

Other multipurposes in here, like home offices, are difficult because you need a large piling system in contained, transparent bins on a bookshelf. This can work, but isn't always the kind of thing you want to stare at in your living room while you relax. Other personality types do a better job with multipurpose living areas because they can hide things without forgetting them. This. Is. Not. You.

Contain the giant tableau

While photographs and books and tchotchkes happen to all types, you are like the DEFCON 2 of décor clutter (we reserve DEFCON 1 for early-stage hoarders). You like to surround yourself with items that remind you of the story of your life and accomplishments . . . and you also have more books than most. This is hardwired, so work with it. Your solutions to book, picture, and tchotchke clutter are almost identical to that of Organic Structures and Smart Structures. You need storage structures large enough to artfully contain all the things with which you surround yourself—think floor-to-ceiling bookshelves. Smart Freedoms usually have a ton of books and trophies reflecting their life's work, and Organic Freedoms have a ridiculous amount of sentimental tchotchkes, photographs, and random things that they adore for equally random reasons. Treat these storage solutions as the giant tableaus that they are. When you're done, whatever items don't fit into this tableau need to find a home somewhere else in your home, in another's home, or in a Later Box.

Keep the best and purge the rest

Making decisions about sentimental items isn't your strong suit, and letting them go pushes against your natural preferences to keep such metaphorical mirrors. We assure you, though, that you can get rid of a bunch of these beloved items after you've reorganized them in a more aesthetically pleasing way—and you will not have to redo this project for ages.

Start by clearing off shelves. As you begin to create your tableaus, organizing and putting stuff back on your shelves to make them look nicer, you'll find low-hanging fruit to purge—books that you can reread electronically or cheap paperbacks you'll never reread. Make sure decorative items are in ideal condition, absolutely adored, and have no other home for which they're better suited.

> **PixieTip!**
>
> Organic Freedoms sometimes even get sentimental about a beat-up paperback—e.g., it reminds you of that summer in 1988. In those instances, take a photo of it and upload it to stumble upon later.

Open storage is ideal

If you are a lucky one with a separate living room, then do your best to contain clutter that creeps in here—books, magazines, or catalogs—in transparent bins that coordinate with the décor, so the room remains inviting. No lids, or you'll forget they exist. As with most storage for you, try to keep it visible, but if what's sitting out will detract from the décor, then you need to either artfully hide it or—even better—replace it with something attractive. It's going to annoy you to entertain grown-ups with a Barbie® townhouse by your side—and you'll probably forget to hide it—but not as much with some cool modern or vintage dollhouse that complements the décor.

You know you're done when your living room is a haven, a respite from the chaos in other parts of your house, and proof that even you can keep a room neat, *especially* if barely anyone ever uses it.

Family- & Living-Room Checklist

- ☐ Clearly delineated living room from family room and other multipurposes, if possible, using a cabinet with doors, opaque bins, hidden printer drawers or shelves, and/or fabric panels
- ☐ Created a U-shape with seating to facilitate conversation, making sure all pieces of furniture are within eighteen inches (46 cm) of each other
- ☐ Found a way to hide, or draw attention away from, the television with storage or art
- ☐ Purchased adequate storage for décor items and any multiuse purposes for the room
- ☐ Purchased enough and large-enough tables so that guests can put drinks down without having to stand up
- ☐ Ditched any old magazines and catalogs, along with tchotchkes and other items you don't love
- ☐ Bought bins for magazines, catalogs, and newspapers
- ☐ Digitized your photo, music, and DVD collections
- ☐ Cleared photo frames off multiuse surfaces and a mounted photo wall gallery
- ☐ Positioned the couch to hide toys and make sure you have enough attractive bin storage for them
- ☐ Purged, relocated, and/or digitized any paperback books in your living area
- ☐ Created an artful and logical tableau of hardcover books, precious tchotchkes, and photographs

CHAPTER TEN

The Master Bedroom

We don't like to use the word *should* outside our motto; but when it comes to your bedroom, it really *should* be an oasis. There's no other way to say it. It's where you go to restore yourself with sleep and relaxation, and frequently we find our clients' bedrooms doubling as anything but, whether there's a messy home office shoved in a corner or clothes draped over an exercise bike, making the room a sad memorial to their failed gym routine. Even the messiest among us have trouble relaxing in that kind of disorder. When space is tight, we understand that rooms have to pull double duty—we both lived in NYC for twenty years, trust us—but do your best to find another spot for the home office or exercise bike and keep your bedroom for sleeping and dressing. It is the easiest way to keep it organized.

UNIVERSAL SOLUTIONS

Master-Bedroom Essentials for *All Types*

- Decimate your wardrobe (it's hard, but it has to be done).
- Buy matching hangers, preferably Huggable Hangers® or a generic version.
- Double your storage with a double hang.
- Mount hooks on the backs of bathroom and closet doors.
- For clothes in drawers, try the trusty fan fold.
- Store shoes on shelves, ideally.
- Purchase two bedside tables and two lamps.
- Have one hamper for dry cleaning or delicates and one for laundry.
- Avoid or camouflage multipurposes.
- If necessary, use underbed storage bins.

It's all about the clothes

The source of bedroom clutter is made very clear when you learn that Americans buy five times as many clothes as we did in 1980. We all know why we keep unworn items: it'll come back in style one day; I'll wear it when I lose weight; I used to love that sweater; it's in perfectly good condition; oh, I wore that for [insert sentimental event]; I bought that [insert insanely expensive, luxurious brand name] two years ago and haven't worn it yet—and so forth. Whatever the reason for keeping garments: if clothes are not worn for two years or more, they're not making it back into the rotation. They're just taking up space, making it harder to find things you *do* wear. Either toss them in a donation bag—mercilessly or thanking each item for their service, Marie Kondo–style—or store them somewhere besides your active closet. Of course, exceptions abound—that fancy party dress you haven't worn in three years, your tuxedo, etc.—but those items are rare.

Clothes residing in your dresser drawers and closet need to be worn regularly. (That's the whole reason they're there, right?) Almost everyone could stand to prune their clothes and accessories. It's never a one-time gig, but if you're brutal about it now, then you can follow one big, clean sweep with smaller ones for years to come.

Take everything out of your closet and drawers, and then methodically go through them one by one. Try on everything—it's annoying but necessary—and then put things into three piles: keep, donate/sell, store. Put the first pile back in your closet. Bag up donations/sales and put 'em in your car or another spot where they will not live for eons. Clothes with stains or holes can be donated—donation centers sell about half of what they receive, and these get repurposed as industrial rags or fillers for couches, mattresses, and so on. Box up any items you can't part with yet (this should be the smallest pile), and put them in storage. You know you're done when you have extra space in your drawers and closet. Now, do the same thing with your jewelry.

> *PixieTip!*
>
> White T-shirts last one year, max, before they need to be recycled. We learned this from our friend and favorite stylist, Lani at **Real Life Style®**. Personally, we push it to two years sometimes, but they never look as good during the second year. (Kelly learned to let go when she sensed pity that she couldn't afford a $5 white T-shirt without pit stains.)
>
> Purging your clothes properly is one of the hardest, most time-consuming organizational activities. Allot the proper time to do it right, and enlist help if you're overwhelmed.

Matching hangers are like magical pixie dust

Matching hangers help you see (and find) your clothes more easily because they're all on the same visual plane, and they are the main reason we all drool over magazine shots of organized closets. Counterintuitively, you want to buy new hangers before decluttering—it's like pre-partying in college, only less fun. Sure, you don't know how many hangers you'll need, but if you wait to buy them until after you declutter, you'll have to take your clothes out of your closet and rehang them *twice*. And why add a step to an already monstrous organization job? For Organics and Smarts, just buying the new hangers can motivate you to purge. Don't worry about getting too many: you want to overbuy because hangers break, you buy more clothes, and a few extra are easily stored on your rod. Get as many as your current total hanging garments, plus ten to twenty extra.

PixieTip!

Get rid of all underwear that's tattered or stained, socks with holes, and socks without matches (you will never find the other one). You will probably have to purchase four to twelve new pairs of identical socks annually, and that's okay: socks are disposable clothing items—not quite paper-plate level, but right behind white T-shirts with pit stains.

The easiest—though not the cheapest—way to get rid of a ton of clothes is to hire a stylist. Good ones are like merciless, decluttering clothing mercenaries who create twice the amount of outfits with half as many clothes.

Double hangs and hooks work miracles

A lucky few of us have a bedroom closet that has a built-in double hang. God bless. Not you? You can easily and cheaply convert a single hang into a double (see Appendix) and thereby double your hanging space. If you want to do it right, you can design an awesome, affordable custom closet using The Container Store's Elfa® system—even if you live in a rental. They're miracle workers—not quite feeding five thousand people with five loaves and two fish, but close. Don't worry about losing long-hang space: most of us (especially men) don't have that many long dresses or jumpsuits. The other bedroom miracle workers are hooks. You can mount at least two hooks on almost any door. If you've got those annoying hollow doors, mount 3M® hooks or use the over-the-door variety. Hooks are a must for Organics and Smarts.

Fan folds are fabulous

Not every type should use drawers to store their clothes, but if you're short on hanging space, then don't just place a stack of folded clothes in your drawers and call it a day. Put your clothes in drawers so you can see each item, fanning out each pile as illustrated. If space is tight, just put the folded stack in vertically, so you can see every shirt when you open the drawer. Not all types *need* to do this, but as we all get older, seeing is remembering.

Fan Fold

Behold: the magical fan fold! You can see every pair of pants you own and easily grab the pair you want.

Shelves aren't just for books

The best storage solution for shoes is shoe shelves. Rows of shoes placed directly on the closet floor end up as a dark cavern of unworn footwear. Only use crappy plastic shoe racks as a temporary measure. The dream closet with row after row of lit, painted shelves and glossy shoes isn't always attainable, but if you install an Elfa closet, include shoe shelves in the design. The shelves are adjustable, so you can have narrow ones for flats and wider ones for tall shoes. Your next best option is stackable, wooden, ready-made shoe shelves. The last resort is a hanging or over-the-door shoe bag.

Keep in mind that shoes don't always have to go inside a closet, as long as they're hidden from view. Most twelve-inch-deep (30.5 cm) bookshelves accommodate shoes quite nicely and are sturdier and longer-lasting than cheap shoe solutions (we've repurposed clients' extra bookshelves more than once). We once even repurposed an unused glass-door curio cabinet in a client's bedroom to store extra shoes. Clear shoe boxes can work, but it's a four-step process to get shoes in and out, and they should never be used if you are an Organic or a Smart.

> **PixieTip!**
>
> To create more space for shoes, place one shoe facing forward and the other shoe facing backward next to each other. It doesn't look as magazine-ready, but neither does having a bunch of shoes strewn across a closet floor.

Bedside tables are not a luxury

Unless you're living alone and want to keep it that way, you need a bedside table with a lamp on both sides. There are a million reasons why you might not have this setup, but only the one we mentioned is rational. The rest are *excuses* (how's that for tough love?). Everyone needs a place to store things where they sleep, whether it's a water glass, your smartphone, or reading material.

We're partial to tables with drawers, so you can store bedside detritus out of sight. At a minimum, make sure any guest-room double bed has two tables. (If not, and your guests tell you they slept really well, one of them is lying because he or she had to put a glass of water on the floor by the bed, tried to get it in the middle of the night, spilled it, had to clean it up, and then couldn't get back to sleep.)

Multiple hampers can stave off extra work

Having a laundry hamper that's separate from your delicates or dry cleaning eliminates the extra step of having to sort through your laundry before every wash, but it also reduces the risk of accidentally ruining an article of clothing that should have gone to the cleaners or in the hand-wash cycle. Think of the countless wool sweaters massacred every year by well-intentioned family members doing someone else's laundry, not realizing it hadn't been separated yet.

A third hamper to consider for your bedroom (or anywhere, frankly) is a donation bin. It's especially helpful to Classic Freedoms and Organic Structures who already have Later Boxes in storage. The "giveaway" hamper is actually an active Later Box that we first began suggesting when Kelly did a purge but wanted to save some of the items for her niece. Now, whenever she's on the fence about keeping something in her bedroom or her house, she puts it in her donation bins and invites visiting friends and family to go through them. Katie got a whole new wardrobe from digging through them once!

No, we're not anti-multipurpose tyrants

Like a dining room, a few personality types can get away with using their master bedroom for multipurposes—as long as it's well camouflaged. Think filing cabinets masquerading as ottomans, a roll-top desk, or a beautiful screen marking off an area. The no-multipurpose rule can be bent for a guest bedroom by all types because they're such a waste of space. But your home office, sewing room, studio, and the like must be behind closed doors or a decorative screen. Half of the population are Classics who will secretly judge any poorly camouflaged, double-duty guest room and hate staying there if it's all commingled. (Although ignoring our advice is a great way to avoid having guests, if that's your ultimate aim.)

Use underbed storage bins

Yes, of course you can get away with not storing stuff under your bed, but if you need to, as many do, then invest in underbed storage bins, preferably with wheels or sliders. It's a dusty, scary mess under there without structure.

Master-Bedroom Closet

1 Mismatched hangers . . . *sigh*. These make clothing look jumbled and harder to sort through.

2 Argh! Every organizer's nightmare: wasted vertical space.

3 Unless it's seasonal storage, sweaters piled high on shelves will end up looking like this unless you're a fastidious Classic—with staff.

4 Where are the purses? Oh, that's right. . . . There's nowhere to put them.

Before

5 Hanging cubbies are terrible for sweaters because retrieval is difficult. These are best saved for kids' rooms; store one outfit per cubby or use the slots for board games.

6 Bottom-of-the-closet mosh pit. Without shelves there are no homes, and without homes, shoes make a mess.

7 See this skirt draped over a hanger? You'll never wear it, because you'll need to iron it first. This right here is an eight- or nine-step process.

8 Can we get a double hang, please? There's much wasted space here.

1 Using a double hang means we can store even more stuff in here.

2 Bins make it easier to reach items on high shelves *without* bringing the whole stack tumbling down.

3 Closed, opaque bins are like coffins for Organics and Smarts; you don't want to look. These are for Classics and Funs only.

4 There's even room for longer clothing to hang in here. Same space but completely maximized.

5 Purses can now reside on a top shelf, held upright by shelf dividers.

After

6 Here, skirts are held firmly on hangers with clips—no ironing necessary. Now wearing a skirt is only a two-step process.

7 Shoe shelves! Divine. You can fit a whole extra pair if you alternate them backward- and forward-facing.

8 Keep boots and everyday shoes on the floor, where there's room. Lesser-used shoes go up on shelves. Always put everyday stuff in easiest-to-access places.

9 Classics and Funs can keep folded shirts in these drawers. Organics and Smarts should endeavor to just keep underwear, socks, and workout gear in here.

10 Organics and Smarts: hang everything you can, including pants and jeans that, unlike skirts, don't get wrinkled when folded over hangers. The more you can see, the more you will wear.

11 Matching hangers make it easy to see what you've got at a glance.

CLASSIC STRUCTURES & CLASSIC FREEDOMS

Master-Bedroom Priorities for *Classics*

- Put purging on your To-Do list, in stages if necessary.
- Use a traditional large box for jewelry storage.
- Most shoe-storage solutions work for you, but make sure you have enough room.
- A secretary desk is best if you're forced to have a home office in here.
- Classic Freedoms: it's okay to keep sentimental clothing, but put it in deep storage or Later Boxes.
- Classic Structures: don't let your practical nature get the better of you—get rid of it!

Make purging clothes a To-Do list item

Well, duh—but it's easy to forget and put the task off forever if it's not marked down. Make this monumental task easier by breaking it into smaller To Dos (buy hangers; prune closet, drawers, shoes; etc.). Doing it all in one go is insanely time-consuming. Give yourself a two-year rule with clothes, although some strict Classics have a one-year rule, and there's nothing wrong with that. Put the task of clearing out your wardrobe and accessories once a year into your calendar, and the task will become minimal. For those of you who do seasonal change-outs, that's the time to purge your clothes. You can color-code your closet; but, more importantly, categorize by garment (e.g., pants, dress shirts, sleeveless shirts, sweaters, jackets, dresses).

You're traditional, so your jewelry storage should be, too

Jewelry storage is best when you use a traditional big jewelry box. These work well for you because you're likely to respect the category areas and maintain the organization within. Use small boxes for overflow and make each box a category—it'll help you remember where things are. We recommend finding a hidden spot behind closed doors to mount hooks for chunky necklaces, though, because the cluttered look of necklaces hanging on a wall by your dresser will annoy you, and traditional jewelry boxes don't do the best job of displaying these items. The caveat is to keep necklaces that tarnish easily inside a box—such as an Izzy Jewel Box®—so they don't oxidize.

All shoe-storage solutions lead back to you

Basically every shoe solution will work for you. You are about the only people who will religiously put away shoes in those shoe bags with tiny compartments. You only get messy with shoes when you lack enough storage space for what you have. Shelves are ideal for you guys because you will religiously put your shoes where there is a home, especially one that's easy to use. If your shoes are getting messy, you don't have enough legitimate homes for them! Solution should be obvious: purge, or expand storage.

If you must, get a secretary desk for this room

Think of a gorgeous dream bedroom overlooking the Adriatic as waves crash below. Chances are, nowhere in that vision is there a massive pile of paper and a utilitarian black printer. You'll sleep better and relax more if you're not in bed staring at office accoutrements. But if reality dictates otherwise, make sure it's a desk that closes up to hide everything, such as a roll-top or a secretary. Ditto

PixieTip!

If you've got more clothes than closet space, change out your clothes seasonally. You'll appreciate the extra room throughout the year. Store the winter or summer clothes in bins under a guest bed, in an extra closet, or in the attic. Or if you're in a big city, use a storage valet service like Box Butler.-® (NYC) or MakeSpace®. These places take your stuff to and from storage, so you don't have to.

While the fan fold is helpful for every type, it's not absolutely necessary for you. Classics will search for a shirt on the bottom of a pile without creating too much of a mess. Just make sure the piles are not too deep—six or more shirts are tough to keep tidy.

for other office furniture. Another option is a desk with big drawers where you drill holes in the back and create hidden sleeping/storage stations for electronics. Any papers on the desk need attractive bins to contain them.

PixieTip!

If you have an extra closet—they are rare but do exist, especially if you are ruthless when pruning your wardrobe or have hired a stylist to do it—hide your office there, so you can close the door on it all.

Saving skinny clothes as motivation to lose weight is a great idea, depending on how much time has passed. Once you've gone through all the hard work to lose the weight, you deserve new clothes that are in style.

Be your own stylist and put together outfits ahead of time, taking photos of the ones you like. It'll help you come up with outfit ideas, and you'll wear more of your wardrobe.

Store sentimental clothing somewhere besides your active closet

Another road bump in decluttering your closet—particularly for Classic Freedoms—is sentimental clothing, whether these are clothes waiting for you to lose weight or that hold special meaning or memories. Part with what you can, and put everything else into a Later Box.

Even men's clothes go out of style

We have found that Classics—usually Structures and males—have the most trouble throwing out unworn or rarely used clothing that is in perfectly good condition. Sometimes the practical part of your brain (they're still wearable, why throw them out?) overtakes the rational part (they're wearable but I never wear them, so there's no reason to keep them). The hard truth is that all clothes go out of style—even men's—so why wear unfashionable clothes when you've only got seven seconds to make a first impression? Keeping unworn or rarely used clothes in your closet because you spent money on them will not right that wrong. Be charitable and let some deserving soul wear these clothes you're not wearing before they've entirely outlived their usefulness.

FUN FREEDOMS & FUN STRUCTURES

Master-Bedroom Priorities for *Funs*

- Purge when you're inspired (e.g., stuff is creeping out of the closet), and preferably with a judgmental companion.
- Color-code to your heart's content.
- Jewelry storage can be a mix of traditional and funky.
- All shoe-storage solutions work for you, so if they're a mess, you need more storage.
- If you must store your office here, hide everything in attractive boxes.
- Fun Freedoms: put sentimental clothing in deep storage or Later Boxes.
- Fun Structures: don't be practical; be critical!

Purge when you're inspired and have a critical companion on hand

Getting rid of clothes on your own is a difficult task. The ideal time is when you're inspired (e.g., you can't take it anymore, or you're moving in with someone). Just make sure to have all your new hangers on hand when you start. You can use the two-year rule, but it doesn't always work for your type. Why? Darned if you guys won't sometimes trot out clothes you haven't worn in two years or more and rock those looks. But nobody bats a thousand. You'll also get rid of more clothes and accessories if you undertake the purge with someone very decisive and a tad judgmental.

PixieTip!

Final decisions are not always "final" to you. You're not indecisive; you just change your mind sometimes. For that reason, we never recommend that you set out an outfit the night before—unless you truly struggle with mornings and don't have much time to prep (or come up with ideas) on a daily basis.

Color-coding was created by you . . . and will only work for you

You're one of the few who will maintain a color-coded system in your drawers and closet if this is important to you. Ditto with jewelry. You can do the regular pile of clothes in a drawer but are one of the few who will take the time to maintain the "fanning" system. Drawer dividers in lingerie and sock drawers will delight you.

Mix traditional and funky jewelry storage, but protect the good stuff

After your jewelry purge, store what's left either in one big jewelry box or in lots of little ones. We find you guys do well with a mix of those two solutions. Closed or open containers—boxes, small platters, shallow bowls—can work. It depends on your preference. Sometimes jewelry makes for beautiful décor right out in the open. Many of you have lots of pretty containers in your house from travels or things that just caught your fancy—use those.

If your shoes are a mess, you need more storage

Every shoe solution will work for you—until you lack enough storage space for what you have. Shelves are perfect because you'll religiously put your shoes where there is a home.

If you must have one in here, make sure your office is tucked away, attractively

If your bedroom is the only spot for a home office, make sure its contents are in attractive, labeled file boxes and bins with lids. Hidden or attractive is the best option for all office equipment—we're talking secretary or wardrobe-type desks that you can close to hide everything. Another great spot for hiding ugly office stuff is an unused closet or portion of a closet where you can mount Elfa shelves to house things. An attractive desk could double as a vanity.

Closets aren't archives

Put things you can't part with yet in a Later Box. Fun Freedoms have more trouble letting go than Fun Structures. Your bedroom isn't for archiving clothes; it's for ones you'll actually wear.

> **PixieTip!**
>
> Make sure your hampers are big enough that you don't have to do laundry *as often.* Obviously, buy some extra underwear, too, so you can make time for more fun in your life.

Channel your inner critic

Fun Structures, especially: channel your hypercritical side when you're pruning your wardrobe. Look for snags, stains, or imperfections on items and get rid of them. You'll know you're done when you have space in your closet and your drawers. If you don't have extra space, then you're not done, and you need to keep going. Remember: the more you get rid of during this session, the less you'll have to do later.

ORGANIC STRUCTURES & SMART STRUCTURES

Master-Bedroom Priorities for *Organic/Smart Structures*

- Hang as much as you can.
- Purge while rehanging items on new, matching hangers.
- Avoid traditional, closed jewelry boxes.
- Do not, we repeat, *do not* put a home office in here.
- Organic Structures: sentimental clothing or stuff you think might be useful someday goes in deep storage or Later Boxes.

You're going to need a lot of hangers

Hang as many clothes as you can, including pants, T-shirts, jeans, and sweaters. This isn't mandatory, but it's incredibly helpful. Remember you have a visual memory, so seeing everything on the same plane in your closet helps you know what you have and where it is. It's tough to find folded clothing in deep drawers, because you forget some are even there, and it's tedious to refold things. We recommend saving drawers for undergarments, socks, and workout gear. Piles of folded clothes on shelves are a great visual but a bitch to maintain—worse than drawers. You pull out one sweater from the middle, a bunch tumble out, and then you have to refold. If you need to do a seasonal change-up, this is the perfect time to schedule the hanger switch. And don't forget to mount hooks.

Buy new hangers, *then* purge

Often you fight us if purging is the first step when reorganizing. That's why we suggest you start reorganizing by rehanging everything on matching hangers first. As you do, you will wonder why you're keeping certain articles of clothing and ditch them rather than rehanging. We suggest purging in this order—unless you find yourself itching to purge, of course.

Beware the traditional, closed jewelry box

Closed jewelry boxes are deadly for you guys. Best to avoid those huge traditional ones. Try solutions like fabric bulletin boards, open bowls, and Izzy Jewel Boxes. We have one client who repurposed a sentimental antique sewing cabinet to hold her jewelry, with necklace stands and additional boxes on top for the stuff she uses most often.

> **PixieTip!**
>
> If you find that you take off earrings, rings, and the like., in a place that is not your proper jewelry home, accept this habit and put a small dish where you tend to do it.

Avoid a home office in the bedroom—at all costs

A home office in this room is a bad idea because of your paper-piling "abilities." Even though you don't notice clutter the way some types do, bedrooms are best for resting—not staring at reminders of things you need to do. You might have tried a secretary or wardrobe desk to hide the clutter, but these don't give you enough space to spread out and make your piles. Your best bet is a decorative screen to hide a big open desk when not in use, especially if you're living with a Classic. Or better yet, put it in the living room or kitchen!

Use Later Boxes or deep storage for stuff you don't wear but can't part with now

Closet purges can be tough for you because there are sentimental items you might want to keep, and then there are many practical reasons to keep things. Now, unworn sentimental items are meant for Later Boxes or somewhere other than the closet. The same goes for clothes you're hoping to fit into, one day. Or tap into your creative side: we have an Organic Structure client who turned her grandmother's wedding dress into wall art.

ORGANIC FREEDOMS & SMART FREEDOMS

Master-Bedroom Priorities for *Organic/Smart Freedoms*

- Schedule a donation or enlist the help of Type A's to start—and finish—the project.
- Make use of donation bins.
- Hang everything except underwear, socks, and loungewear.
- Shoes go on shelves and the closet floor.
- Jewelry storage must be out in the open, or you'll never wear it.
- NO home office in here.
- Organic Freedoms: Later Boxes and deep storage may be your saving grace.

Starting and finishing are equally daunting

One of the toughest things about purging clothes and accessories is finding the inspiration to do it in the first place. Then once you start, it's so overwhelming that finishing can be tough. It's not as easy as "Put it on your To-Do list, and it'll get done" as it is for others (Katie still hasn't finished putting things away a year after moving into a new home). Obviously, you'll start the project

PixieTip!

If your closet is stuffed to the gills, your best bet is to do a brutal purge (as in, with a stylist) because a seasonal change-up isn't a great solution for you (one more thing to put on your mental To-Do list that may or may not get done). If you can't do this type of purge, then you've got to bite the bullet and force yourself to do a seasonal change-up.

Organics: don't overthink where you're donating or recycling clothes. It's all better than ending up in the landfill.

when you're motivated (after reading this section, for example!) or you have a deadline, but it's hard to create a deadline to finish clothes closets and drawers. (It's not like you're going to have a cocktail party in your closet.) One way to create a deadline is to schedule a clothing pickup with the Salvation Army. Another way to finish this project is to empty your closet and drawers onto your bed so there's no rest until you're done (although we've known Organic and Smart Freedoms who have then shoved this project onto the floor in order to sleep). For most of you, it'll be enough incentive to finish before bedtime that day. One of the best ways to finish is to do it with a mean friend who keeps a tight schedule, such as a Classic (they're basically walking, breathing deadlines). Hiring a stylist or an organizer will have the same impact.

Donation bins are your friends

Whatever you do to motivate yourself, don't leave donations lingering in your house. Pack 'em up in trash bags, and, if you're going to recycle, put them in your car and donate them the very day you finish while you're still "in the zone." Otherwise, they'll be there for a long time, negating the whole point of the purge. Going forward, keep a small donation bin in your car, so you can dump things from smaller purges whenever you randomly pass by a clothing-donation container.

Hang everything (well, almost)

When you're done pruning your clothes, hang everything up, including stuff most people put in drawers (e.g., T-shirts, jeans, shorts). The only items in your drawers should be socks, underwear, and loungewear. This is mandatory, because you have a visual memory, and seeing everything in one glance means you'll actually remember these garments. A double-hang closet is also mandatory, because this storage method requires a lot of hanging space! In addition, hanging things is faster than folding—and refolding—them. Our Pixie Mantra of *"Reduce organization procedures as close to one step as possible"* was written expressly with you in mind. Our Universal Solution for Huggable Hangers also creates more hanging room; and if you want to get creative, you can retrofit a deep cabinet that's about twenty-two inches (56 cm) deep and forty inches (102 cm) tall with a hanging rod to act as a less-obtrusive wardrobe with a surface for jewelry boxes and other small items.

Shoes go on shelves (and the closet floor)

Your natural shoe M.O. is to kick them off wherever you are when it occurs to you. But, even if you live alone, shoes need proper homes on shoe shelves. Chances are that you wear the same ones a lot, so shoe shelves are only for gently used shoes, like high heels, formal shoes, summer sandals when it's snowing, and boots when the sun's hot. When you manage to find your way to your closets to take off your shoes, kick them off on the floor, close the door, and don't worry about putting them nicely away on shelves. (Umm, hello—you should congratulate yourself for getting your shoes *in* there in the first place!) But since you'll have already set up a double hang for hanging all your clothing, there might not be enough room for all your shoes to be strewn across your closet floor. In this scenario, get a bin no more than six inches (15 cm) deep for dumping shoes near your closet (if it's too deep, you'll forget about the shoes on the bottom).

Hooks, hooks, hooks, and yes: even more hooks!

Put hooks *everywhere* to hold clothes you usually drape over a chair or other furniture. Placing a garment on a hook uses the same amount of steps as putting it on a chair, but has the added benefit of not rendering the chair useless. Those draped clothes are the visual result of delayed decision-making: Is it dirty? Should I fold it up? Am I going to re-wear it tomorrow? Every type does it, but you do it more often. Mount hooks on the backs of doors, in your closet, or on your wall. Place them where you tend to naturally undress, employing another of our Pixie Mantras: *"Formalize your natural organizational tendencies."* You might not like the aesthetic, but a coat rack on a wall looks nicer than a pile of clothes on a chair!

Have hampers that are big enough to hold all of your clothes until laundry day; don't use the lid; and *never* buy a hamper with a connected top—we swear you'll pile clothes on top of an empty hamper!

No jewelry boxes

Closed jewelry boxes are deadly for your jewelry, in terms of getting playtime—you're never going to wear earrings that are in a box within a box. It's best if it's all out in the open. Think bulletin boards, open bowls, hooks mounted on a wall, and so on. If you don't already have attractive bowls, they're easy to find online at Etsy® or Pier 1®. If you have jewelry that tarnishes, get an Izzy Jewel Box. Store jewelry where you tend to take it off, with perhaps a temporary home where you put the jewelry you wear more often and a larger permanent home for nicer pieces on top of a dresser or vanity.

No home office at all

A home office in this room is a major *don't* for you guys. It's got disaster written all over it. Plus, you can work anywhere, so we're positive you can find an alternate room to house a home office. Who wants to think about work or stare at a messy pile of paper when trying to sleep or relax in bed? Yes, not even you!

Later Boxes are your lord and savior

It almost goes without saying, but store sentimental stuff you can't part with in Later Boxes or deep storage.

Master-Bedroom Checklist

- ☐ Took all clothing and accessories out of closets, drawers, and boxes, dividing them into "keep," "sell/donate," and "store" categories (or hired a stylist)
- ☐ Sold, donated, or stored clothing and accessories that are never or rarely used
- ☐ Got rid of stained clothes, tattered underwear, socks with holes, and socks with no matching pair
- ☐ Bought matching (Huggable) hangers
- ☐ Got some form of a double hang if you didn't already have one
- ☐ Mounted hooks on the backs of bathroom or closet doors, if necessary
- ☐ Used a vertical or fan fold for clothing items that must go in drawers
- ☐ Bought enough shelving and shoe bags or boxes to store all shoes
- ☐ Made sure the bedroom has two bedside tables and two lamps
- ☐ Bought separate hampers for regular laundry, delicates, donations, and/or dry cleaning
- ☐ Relocated home office or bought appropriate, attractive office furniture, storage, and/or screens for this room
- ☐ Purchased underbed storage bins and appropriate jewelry containers
- ☐ Found yourself with more storage than you currently need (congratulations!!!)

CHAPTER ELEVEN

The Bathroom

Bathrooms are onerous for everyone to keep tidy because they hold so many small products, and many of us only have one deep under-sink cabinet—or at best a few drawers and a medicine cabinet. God help you if you don't have a medicine cabinet, or someone watched too much HGTV and installed a pedestal sink—they may sell homes, but they sure make it impossible to *store* anything in there!

UNIVERSAL SOLUTIONS

Bathroom Essentials for *All Types*

- Purge expired and rarely used toiletries and medicines.
- Avoid pedestal sinks—seriously.
- Purchase/install under-sink pullout drawers, under-sink bins, and/or shallow wall shelves.
- Limit shampoo and conditioner sets to three.
- Mount chrome shower caddies or shelves.
- A medicine cabinet with narrow, shallow bins is ideal for corralling small, essential items.
- Sample products must be easy to retrieve.
- Get hooks for robes and bath toys.

Trash it

Don't let the size of these rooms deceive you: bathrooms harbor a lot of trash. They can take us half a day to organize, not including the thirty minutes of measuring and time to find the right storage products. Luckily, most of this purged stuff can't be donated, so you can trash or recycle almost everything without guilt. Break the room down into three areas—medicine cabinet, shower/bath, sink storage—and then start throwing things out. Check expiration dates and get rid of anything you haven't used in a year or two. What's left is meant for your daily routine, plus a few seasonal, first-aid, and wellness items. We had an Organic Structure client who purged before we came over but decided to keep a bottle of beloved hairspray from the '80s in case she ran out of her regular hairspray (because who wouldn't want to put thirty-year-old chemicals on their hair in a pinch?).

When purging, remember that all personality types can have strong feelings about their toiletries;

don't throw things out without permission or risk World War III. This is especially important for Smarts, Classic Structures, and Fun Structures to remember. We put our clients' stuff in a "suggested trash" bag and let them riffle through it for things they want to keep. Everyone's medicine cabinet has leftover meds from surgeries or illnesses—"just in case I get sick again or need real painkillers," or even "I'll keep this Cipro® in case there's some airborne bacterial plague"—but by the time any of this comes to pass, you'll have seen a doctor and gotten the appropriate medicine (or learned the hard way that your Cipro lost its effectiveness a long time ago). Trashing them is an easy way to make space.

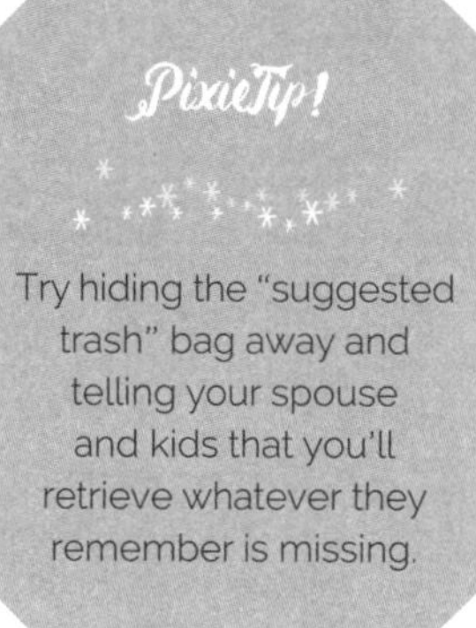

Pedestal sinks are for sadists

Pedestal sinks are purely for powder rooms. You'll need and use under-sink storage. Units with almost all drawers are best, as they provide immediate structure without much effort on your part. But if you don't have drawers, install an under-sink pull-out drawer and corral smaller items in matching bins. If a full pullout drawer isn't possible—often pipes and valves prevent it—install a narrow drawer on one side and put bins on the other. We liken organizing a bathroom to a jigsaw puzzle or a game of Tetris®—similar to kitchen drawers. If you need more storage, mount shallow wall shelves in an unobtrusive spot, buy a narrow bookshelf, or get a larger medicine cabinet, adjusting the height of the shelves to maximize storage.

Limit shampoos and conditioners with chrome caddies or shelves

Keep your shampoos and conditioners down to three sets. Yes, you heard us: *three.* Invest in chrome bath/shower caddies or shelves that are at eye level. Shelves add structure and remind you to keep the bottle count low. Unless your tub is lined in a precious stone, like marble, use silicone to mount a shelf, which won't damage most surfaces if you need to remove it later (Katie found a special cement from Germany that won't damage *any* kind of stone, in fact). If nothing else, get a vertical tension-rod caddy or the kind that hangs over the shower head.

Medicine cabinets are a must

Medicine cabinets are not ideal storage for medicine, as the humidity can be damaging, but they're the best way to keep your daily products at your fingertips. Invest in small, narrow, shallow drawer bins—to organize the contents of this cabinet into distinct groups (e.g., makeup, skin care, hair products). You can even use some of your sentimental mugs to corral makeup brushes and toothbrushes.

In an ideal world, you should keep everything but soap and brushes inside a medicine cabinet so your countertops are not covered with detritus. You need space to work. This is why medicine cabinets are essential for bathroom organization, as kitchen cabinets are for kitchens. If you don't have a medicine cabinet or have a tiny one, then keep your daily toiletries in attractive bins out on shelves as a last resort.

> **PixieTip!**
>
> We keep pills and vitamins in upper kitchen cupboards, away from the heat of the stove, because it frees up space in the bathroom. Many medications need to be taken with food, after all.
>
> Travel much? Keep a separate kit of toiletries in your suitcase to save space in a crowded bathroom.

Sample products are insidious

Beauty-product samples are the bane of our existence when we're tackling bathrooms. Some people *love* their sample products, and if that's you, we're not going to tell you to throw them out. We will tell you, however, that no matter what your PixieType, they must be organized in bins and easy to retrieve—or you'll never use them. Oh, and they expire, too.

Hampers and hooks are bathroom saviors

Hampers in this room—space allowing—are awesome if you or others take off dirty clothes in here, and especially if you have children. Have at least one or two hooks on the back of the bathroom door so that you can hang nightgowns or robes if you're a morning shower person. Speaking of children, get a plastic sieve-type tote to gather bath toys in one place and hang it inside the bathtub on a large Command™ hook that can easily be taken down once the children outgrow the toys.

CLASSIC FREEDOMS & CLASSIC STRUCTURES

Bathroom Priorities for *Classics*

- Remember: toiletries and medicine go bad.
- Jerry-rigged solutions are not the sturdiest.
- Tuck things away in matching bins (aesthetics matter).

You don't need that hair gel from 1985

You tend to keep things on hand for just-in-case moments, which means there are those among you who have medical products from the year 2000 (or earlier). Ditch these, as their efficacy is questionable at best. Your other struggle with decluttering in here is holding on to products that you bought but never used. Be honest with yourself: if you're in doubt over whether you're going to use it, then throw it out. As for beauty products, let go of untouched remnants. Sure, you went through that phase when you used mousse instead of hair gel, but the tiny bit at the bottom of the bottle is not worth the real estate it's taking up.

Jerry-rigged solutions are *not* meant to be long-term

Resist getting clever with shower-tub storage. We once discovered a Classic who had mounted a horizontal tension rod up high opposite the shower curtain rod and then hung buckets to hold a plethora of shampoos and conditioners.

Then we saw it on Pinterest, too! There's a reason this solution isn't for sale at Pottery Barn: there's an 80-percent chance it will all come crashing down. Take the time (and money) to install proper shower-tub storage.

Hide and match

Visible clutter is unsettling to you, so you'll be happier if you can hide toothbrushes and toothpaste in your medicine cabinet. If you have to store items on open shelves, get opaque bins that coordinate with your décor. Avoid containers with lids if they're within cabinets—it's one step too many to ask of a human for getting a bath product.

Hide toilet paper (behind your toilet doesn't count). If you don't have room in a cabinet, invest in a closed TP canister that floats your boat. A toilet tank should never have anything on top of it! Also, get a matching toilet-bowl cleaner brush that is closed and contained. It's never okay to have a non-hidden plunger next to the toilet. Nasty.

Everyone loves the aesthetic pleasure of matching items, but this brings you more joy than it does to others; so even in the utilitarian bathroom, invest in bins that match, even if they are hidden away. Don't reuse tops of boxes and random bits on hand to organize (yes, we know it's thrifty, and even Classic Kelly is guilty of doing so in hidden spots). For you to adore your home, practicality can't always beat aesthetics. They've got to work together, seamlessly.

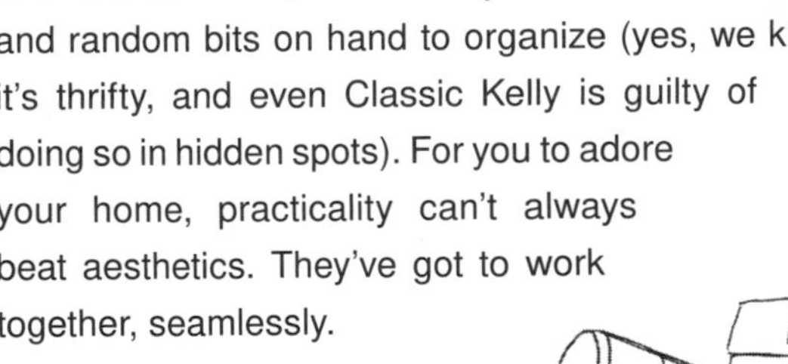

Bathroom

1 Would you even remember there's a curling iron in here?

2 This hair dryer can't easily get lots of use, can it? Retrieval matters.

3 This could be any personality type's neglected, unpurged, overstuffed, under-sink bathroom storage. Even a Classic's—gasp!

4 How many things would you have to move to get to the light bulbs back here?

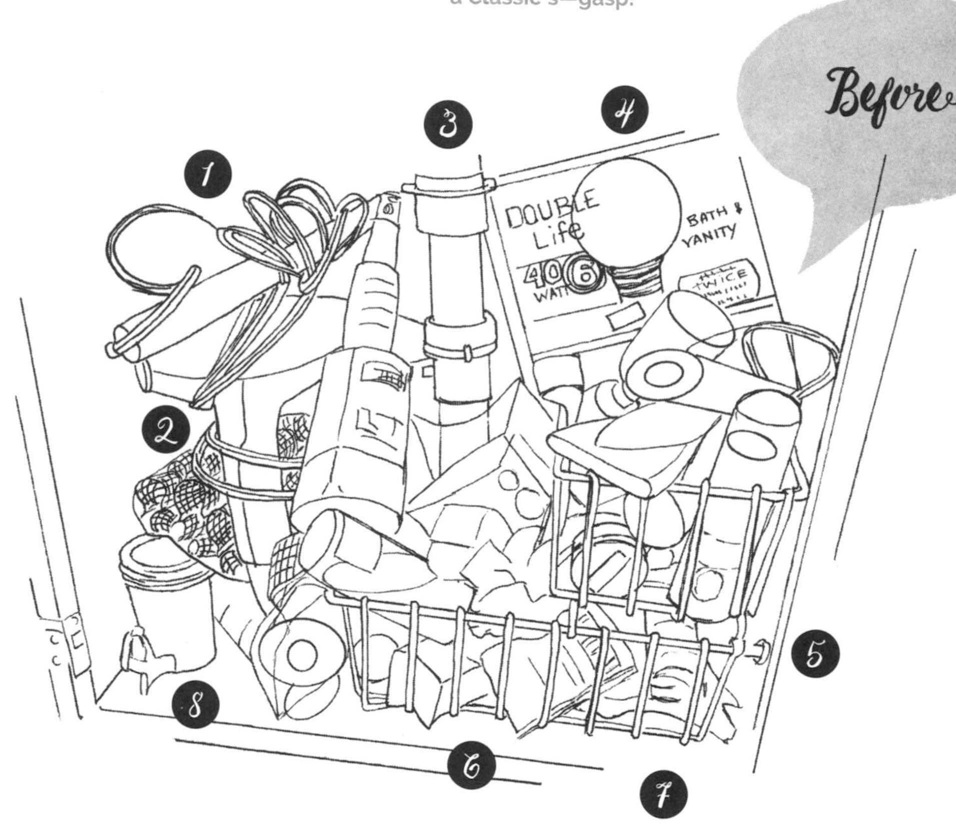

5 Here are some old, neglected organizing drawers that are designed to pull out but don't anymore thanks to being overstuffed.

6 The items stored here are too small for the structure and are falling through the cracks. Under-sink storage needs big items, or small items contained in small bins.

7 What's in here? It's unlikely that anyone actually knows.

8 Is that an old coffee cup?

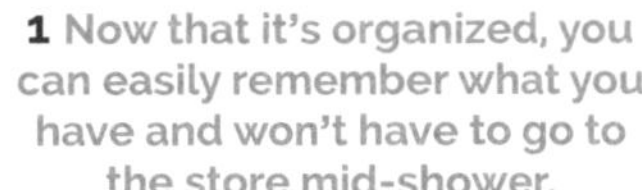

1 Now that it's organized, you can easily remember what you have and won't have to go to the store mid-shower.

2 Use small bags for holding small items, like hair clips and shoe-polish supplies. This system is perfect for Classics and Funs. Some Organics and Smarts may forget what's inside unless they use the contents regularly; it might be helpful to add labels.

After

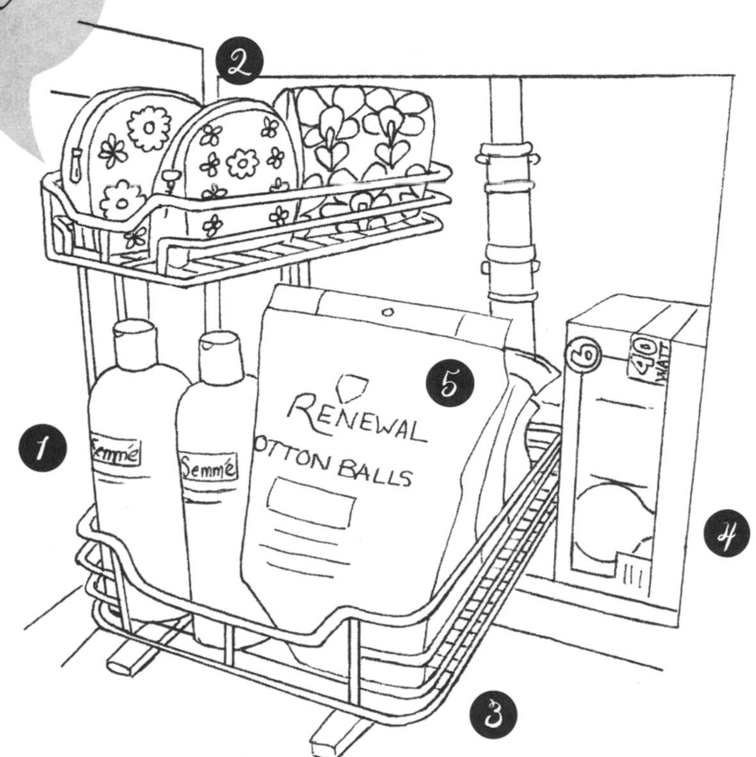

3 Here's a nice, sturdy, attractive pullout drawer solution that actually works. Buying a new organizer is a great impetus for Organics and Smarts to purge and finally get rid of that thirty-year-old hair spray.

4 Keep storage items close to where they're used, like the specialty bulbs for that over-sink lighting.

5 Under-sink storage is perfect for bulky items, like cotton balls, toilet paper, oversize shampoo and conditioner, etc.

FUN FREEDOMS & FUN STRUCTURES

Bathroom Priorities for *Funs*

- Make purging a contest.
- Jerry-rigged solutions are no good.
- Corral things in attractive, coordinating bins or bowls.
- Keep cleaning products readily accessible.

Turn the purge into a game

Especially if your bathroom purge yield is sparse, try the clutter game we learned from Barbara Kingston in her book *Clear Your Clutter with Feng Shui*. Challenge yourself to throw out an item in here once a day. Do it for thirty days (or whenever you remember), and voilà! Your purge is done.

No jerry-rigging for you

You are like Classics when it comes to trouble in the bathroom, sometimes choosing practicality over aesthetics. Resist your jerry-rigging nature and buy a few proper storage bins and products that we suggest in the universal section that fit the space. We had one totally normal Fun client who used a cardboard box cutout to place over his bathroom window to create privacy. We took one look and thought "Crack den. Definitely a crack den." Hardware stores sell privacy film you can cut out and put over a window. Privacy and light—what a concept!

Aesthetics matter, even in here

If you have to store items on an open shelf, coordinating opaque bins or bowls makes things look neater. Of course you can mix and match what you have on hand with new stuff, but if it's ugly, it needs to be behind closed doors or drawers.

Make sure that everything you have out on the sink is attractively corralled, perhaps with a coordinating mug or glass. Hide toilet paper, toilet-bowl brushes, plungers, and the like. You're the kind of people who can come up with a fun solution, like tossing a handful of TP rolls in large attractive bins.

Clean on the fly

Keep your bathroom clean by having your go-to bath cleaners and paper towels unobtrusively handy for quick cleanings when you notice it's super gross. Taking care of something amiss when you see it is one of your strengths, and having cleaning products handy feeds right into these natural instincts. Plus you've eliminated the need to schedule a bathroom cleaning. Woohoo!

ORGANIC STRUCTURES & SMART STRUCTURES

Bathroom Priorities for *Organic/Smart Structures*

- Buy storage, then purge (brutally).
- If absolutely necessary, let discarded items sit in a garbage bag for a week and rescue anything you can't bear to part with.
- Use transparent bins and organizers for small items.
- Only large items go under the sink.
- Everyday essentials should be visible.
- Hooks are better than towel racks.

Your bathroom clutter would shock half the population

What's a shocking amount of clutter to you is roughly a hundred times worse than a Classic's idea of horrendous clutter. We joke, but you have more purging to do than most. Blame it on your "big picture" brain that you don't notice the growing mess as much as others. It's usually hidden away in a cabinet or a drawer, and "out of sight" = "out of mind."

Start organizing by investing in bins or under-sink pullout shelves. Sometimes the act of creating storage can give you the impetus you need to start purging. Be brutal. You know you are doing it right when you are uncomfortable or having a full-on anxiety attack. In the latter scenario, put everything that *should* be discarded in a plastic garbage bag. Let it sit for a week—like a Later Box on speed—and then rescue whatever you wish you hadn't thrown out. The chances of your having a serious attachment to many toiletries is low . . . we think!

Bins within bins

You will tend to have one big drawer filled with just makeup and think it's organized. Like with like, right? But how much time do you waste trying to find the one eyeliner that is sharpened because you can't find the eyeliner sharpener in your big ol' drawer of makeup?

When it comes to the bathroom, push away your preference for seeing the forest, and instead look at all the individual trees and leaves. Purchase transparent drawer organizers and use them. There are lots of little products in here that need distinct homes, or it's tough to find them on a daily basis. Bins do wonders, even if the categories get muddled eventually.

Under-sink cabinets are like black holes

Be wary of storing a lot of small items under your sink, or you'll never find anything. The minute you close a door on something that is hard to get to, the black hole starts to grow. As a result, this area is best suited for big, obvious items like bulk toilet-paper rolls, bags of cotton balls, or bulk shampoo purchases—especially if you can't fit a pullout shelf drawer down there. You would be lost without a medicine cabinet for everyday products. Sure, it hides things, but it's shallow and at your eye level.

Keep the essentials visible

You can ignore the sparse, ideal countertop concept that we painted earlier, but limit surface space to daily essentials only. Get glass or clear acrylic matching containers for Q-tips and cotton balls (or equivalents) that are out on sink countertops. There are also specially designed containers to tuck away hair dryers and curling irons on the back of a lower cupboard door. Lids are unnecessary on bins in cabinets or on counters. If you're using open shelving in here, you may be annoyed by the cluttered look, but deep, opaque baskets or bins won't work for you.

Towel racks are for idiots

Swap your towel racks for hooks. They make it much easier to hang up wet towels. The extra steps necessary to keep towels looking neat on a towel rack are not worth the effort. Save your energy to keep your other toiletries organized. Mount enough hooks for each person—plus a few extra for robes, etc.—so you can hang up those towels in one step.

ORGANIC FREEDOMS & SMART FREEDOMS

Bathroom Priorities for *Organic/Smart Freedoms*

- Bathrooms are your organizational Moby Dick.
- Keep basics visible but contained.
- Under-sink storage is a bad idea for most things.
- Towel racks and lids are to be avoided.
- Hampers and hooks are lifesavers.
- Keep cleaning products in here.

Thar she blows!

This might be the toughest room in the house for you to keep tidy. It's full of your organizing arch-nemesis: *detail* (i.e., tiny products that all need homes). Do yourself a favor and *never* take free samples. Just. Don't. Give up on catching that white whale—the perfectly organized bathroom—and perhaps settle for a clean bathroom in which you can find most things when you need them.

Keep basics out on the counter

Keep your daily bathroom basics out on the counter, as a little clutter doesn't usually bug you. Use acrylic see-through containers for things like cotton balls and Q-tips. No need for lids. If you don't have a medicine cabinet, please get one. It's the only way you'll avoid ending up with *everything* on the counter.

Corral small items in drawers with small transparent bins. It's especially important to do this if you can't fit a pullout drawer under the sink. For this space, stick to infrequently used larger items. Never store anything under the sink that you're going to use frequently—you're not going to take a bin out of a deep under-sink hiding spot and then put it away daily. Something's going to disrupt you in the middle of using it, and then that bin will become a permanent fixture on your sink, radiator, or toilet tank. (This rule doesn't apply to bins in an eye-level medicine cabinet.)

Towel racks are like kryptonite to you

Replace them with hooks for those wet towels. Mount as many hooks as there are people using the bathroom, plus a few more for good luck. An open hamper for dirty clothes and towels is essential in here. No lid. An open wastebasket is also essential. Of course, a covered one looks nicer, but you've got to make life easier for yourself since you're already pushing up against all your natural preferences in order to keep this room and its myriad details from overwhelming you. Covered TP canisters are a bad idea—you'll never know when you're running low—but you can get away with a covered plunger and toilet-bowl scrub next to the toilet.

PixieTip!

Avoid mixing TP storage with small-item storage under the sink. You are apt to toss the toilet paper in willy-nilly and scatter the small stuff, making it chaotic for a long time.

Make cleaning easy

A parting shot to keep your bathroom from devolving into a germy landfill is to store your bathroom cleaner in here for quick cleanings when you notice that your sink or toilet is super gross. Taking care of something amiss when you see it comes naturally to you.

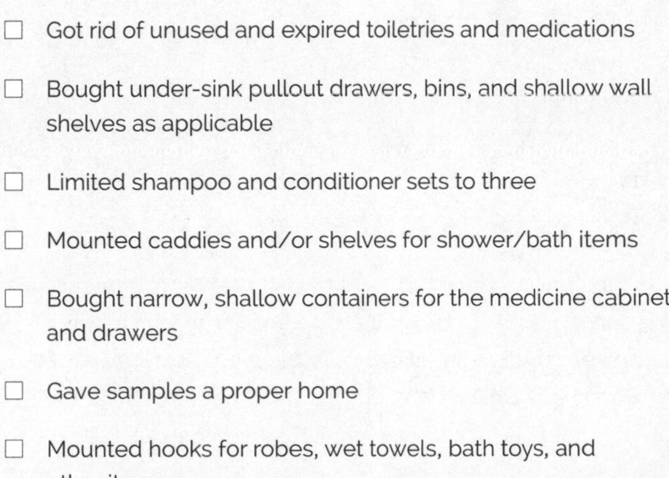

Bathroom Checklist

- ☐ Got rid of unused and expired toiletries and medications
- ☐ Bought under-sink pullout drawers, bins, and shallow wall shelves as applicable
- ☐ Limited shampoo and conditioner sets to three
- ☐ Mounted caddies and/or shelves for shower/bath items
- ☐ Bought narrow, shallow containers for the medicine cabinet and drawers
- ☐ Gave samples a proper home
- ☐ Mounted hooks for robes, wet towels, bath toys, and other items

CHAPTER TWELVE

The Kids' Rooms and Playroom

Kids have personalities just like adults, but even the neatest kids have better things to do than clean up their bedrooms or playroom. There is a great book called *Nurture by Nature: Understand Your Child's Personality Type: And Become a Better Parent* by Paul D. Tieger and Barbara Barron-Tieger that can help you figure out your kid's personality type, so you know what kind of child you're dealing with. Every type who lives in disorder is going to give up trying to keep it neat if there's no organizational infrastructure, though. Our recommendations here are for how *you* can best deal with their messes—as you will need to in their earliest years. As they get older and can help out more, knowing you have a fastidious Classic Structure on your hands or a messy Smart Freedom will then assist you in finding the best way to teach them how to organize.

UNIVERSAL SOLUTIONS

Kids' Rooms and Playroom Essentials for *All Types*

- Purge frequently and with your kids . . . if possible.
- Set up a large floor-to-ceiling toy storage system.
- Get matching or coordinating bins for toys.
- Labels that combine words and visuals are ideal.
- Have double hangs in their closets.
- Get matching hangers that are small enough for their small clothes.
- Set up a storage system for outgrown clothes and keepsakes.
- Place sentimental pieces in deep storage or digitize them.

Purge, purge, purge!

Toys multiply faster than rabbits, so purging is a frequent necessity. While we would love to say to everyone: "Do it before the holidays every year," who in the heck has extra free time then?? Not the two of us. We'll delve into purging by personality type, but ideally involve your kids, and in the process teach them about making tough decisions and charity (we said *ideally*). You'll pull out your hair doing it this way with most of them, though, so it's usually easier to purge toys when kids are not around, especially if you know which toys they adore. Set aside any toys you're unsure about, rather than donating or recycling them right away. Start with toys that are too young for them, broken toys, toys missing pieces, and toys you hate. Picturing a kid in a foster agency playing with your kids' toys will make you feel better about donating anything that was sitting unloved on a shelf or in a basket.

Kids will learn to clean up if there are labeled homes for all their stuff. After a day of play, all the stuff on the floor can be overwhelming for them, and even a two-year-old will help if you do it with them.

Everyone needs more toy storage than they think

Even if you throw one toy out every day, we swear it won't be enough. The biggest mistake that parents make, regardless of type, is buying ad hoc bins as the toys begin to seep out. Like books and tchotchkes in living areas, toys need a "big picture" floor-to-ceiling storage system taking up at least one wall of a toy room, if not more. Depending on your type, closed drawers, cabinets, open shelving, or bins within this big structure will keep things contained. Just make sure to have any heavy furniture triple-secured to the wall for safety by a professional; kids always climb.

Get matching or coordinating bins for toys

Without bins, you have no homes for these toys, and as much as all of us would love to have our children put their toys or materials neatly back on trays, upon shelves, don't waste your precious time keeping it in order. Trust us: we've tried it, and we collectively have over twenty years of Montessori education. If we can't do it, then no one can.

Bins make it easy to put toys away quickly—no lining up or making sure toys look nice. But if they're a mishmash of plastic bins and baskets that you've collected over the years, it's not going to *look* organized, even if they each hold different categories. We'll get into how each PixieType needs different kinds of bins for toys, but *everyone* needs to get matching or coordinating bins. Put large toys on the floor so kids can pull them out on their own. Reserve high shelves for the toys you don't want kids to access on their own (e.g., games with small pieces, puzzles, arts-and-crafts supplies).

Visuals with words make great labels for kids

Without labels, what is obviously a bin for "Animals" or "Cars" will eventually become a disorganized mess. The best labels for kids have laminated visuals and words. They are a pain to do, but it will help kids participate in the cleanup before they can read. Plain gift tags work on baskets, but sticky labels and label-machine tape can work, too.

They will need double hangs in their closets, with matching hangers

Short hangs are almost mandatory for kids' closets because, unless they're Benjamin Button, they're short. If you have a long hang in here, half of their closet is wasted storage space. We use Elfa closets so clients can change things up as the kids grow. When we're keeping it low-budget, we get a double-hang rod to transform half the closet and then add hanging sweater cubbies or shoe cubbies off to the side. When we do an Elfa redesign, we add shelves above or below a short or double hang. We use shelves for a variety of things—shoes, toys, bins, books—depending on the room's needs. As for what height is best for a hanging rod, it depends on whether you want the kids to be able to access their clothes or the shelves on their own!

Mini-matching Huggable Hangers® for kids follow the same principle as for adults. It helps you (and them) see all of the clothes in there because they're on the same visual plane. Buy *at least* twelve more than you need per kid.

Buy bins for outgrown clothes and keepsakes

Kids grow out of clothes faster than you have time to properly store them or decide what to keep, what to give to friends and family, and what to donate. When they're babies, it happens at breathtaking speed. We suggest having a large bin in their closet to make this frequent pruning easier. When the bin fills up, go through it, put in deep storage what you want to preserve, and donate/recycle the rest. Another spot for these bins is under the bed. Growing out of clothes happens less frequently as kids age, so eventually you can keep the bins in storage to free up space in their room. Keep empty bins stacked in your storage area for these clothes.

PixieTip!

Folding clothes is about as easy for kids as origami. Ever seen a drawer after a child has looked for something in there? It's a war zone. When folding kids' clothes, roll them up like the military does and place them side by side. It'll be easier for kids to see what's in there and re-roll on their own.

Another bin that's nice to have is one for keepsakes. Whether it's special correspondence, baby jewelry, or random items that don't fit in albums or are awaiting such a project, these need a specific, permanent home. Get one for yourself while you're at it.

Prized artwork and schoolwork go in physical bins or digital albums

Kelly still remembers how over-the-moon she was the time her eldest brought home his first masterpiece. Now she sighs when he brings home yet another. Some of you can throw it away; others don't have the heart. You'll know which mind-set you have almost immediately upon receiving the sixth or seventh masterpiece. We all become more ruthless as time passes. The bigger your heart when it comes to kids' artwork, the bigger the storage bin needs to be. Files don't work. Depending on your personality type, you can mix schoolwork in with artwork or file it like you do other paper. For those more ruthless among you but not entirely "heartless," take photos to make an album and ditch the actual work. There's also a digitizing app that creates detailed books of your snapshots. Smart, Classic, and Fun Structures? Unless your children end up like you, they might judge you harshly as adults for not keeping any of their childhood work. Digitize the cream of the crop, with maybe a few physical exceptions.

> **PixieTip!**
>
> Keep an active bin for kids' art and schoolwork in the home office, and another bigger one in deep storage. When you transfer from active to deep storage, quickly riffle through this bin to see if there's anything that doesn't really need to be saved for posterity.

CLASSIC FREEDOMS & CLASSIC STRUCTURES

Kids' Rooms and Playroom Priorities for *Classics*

- Decide what level of tidiness you can live with, then routinize it.
- Opaque bins and cabinet doors are best, especially if toys share space in family or living rooms.
- Schedule a biannual or annual purge.

Clean up, clean up, everybody, everywhere!

The daily mess of small children is particularly difficult for you. It's the constant change of their growing bodies and needs and constant onslaught of more and more stuff. Luckily, you're good at discipline and routines, which kids thrive under; so rely on those strengths, and childhood will slide by faster than you could ever want.

Figure out how often you need these rooms to be tidy for your sanity (morning/night) and then let go in between, lest you go mad. Otherwise you'll waste countless hours tidying up after people who seem like wild animals, unless you are the special Classic who can close a door on a mess and forget about it. We have one Classic client who keeps kids' toys confined to their playroom and bedrooms, while another insists on having a spotless, tidy house throughout the day. Guess which one of them goes to sleep after midnight most nights? But if you can't ignore hidden messes, then train your kids early to clean up after themselves.

Hidden is divine

If toys have to reside in areas without a door, lidded toy boxes along with matching and opaque open bins on shelves or the floor are your best bets for creating the most Zen. But you'll be happiest if toys have one main home, with maybe a satellite station somewhere, instead of having things strewn randomly all around the house.

Playroom

1 Is this huge television teetering on a too-small cabinet tethered to the wall? *This* is how you get on the evening news in a very bad way.

2 If you let a three-year-old near this stack of games, we promise you that the games will be dismantled in seconds and you'll never play them again.

3 This wall is crying out for structure and a brilliant, vertical-storage plan. Hold on—Pixies to the rescue!

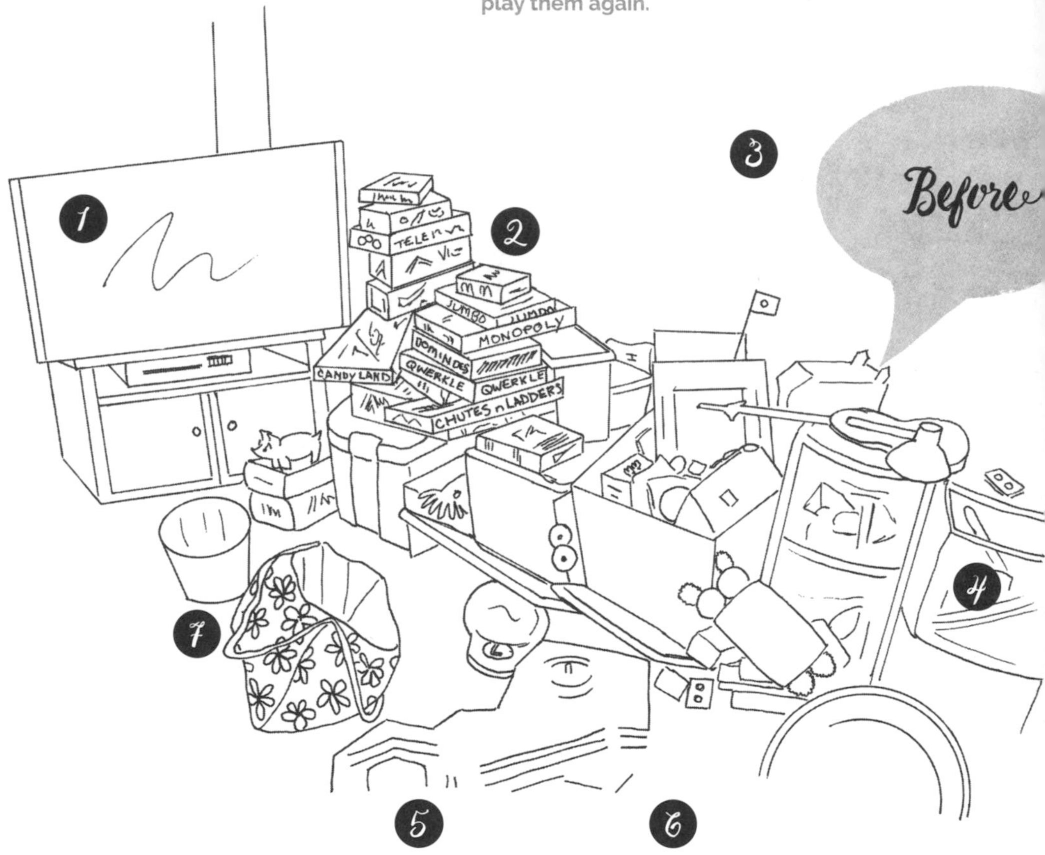

4 This is what Katie's side of the room looked like to Kelly when they were growing up.

5 Child Katie—plus most kids—would never know how to put her toys away in this mess.

6 We think this is too cluttered for even a child to play in.

7 Here's one lonely bin, unused because nothing else matches and there are no categories.

1 The best way to de-emphasize a big television is to surround it. Also, make sure it's securely attached to the wall, so kids won't get hurt.

2 It's best to keep the books you read with them up high, so they don't add to play.

3 Keep small toys like games and puzzles you prefer to supervise—or at least have control over—completely out of reach and unnoticeable.

4 Open, clear bins are best for Organics and Smarts. They really don't *need* to be labeled, but if they become miscellaneous, label them.

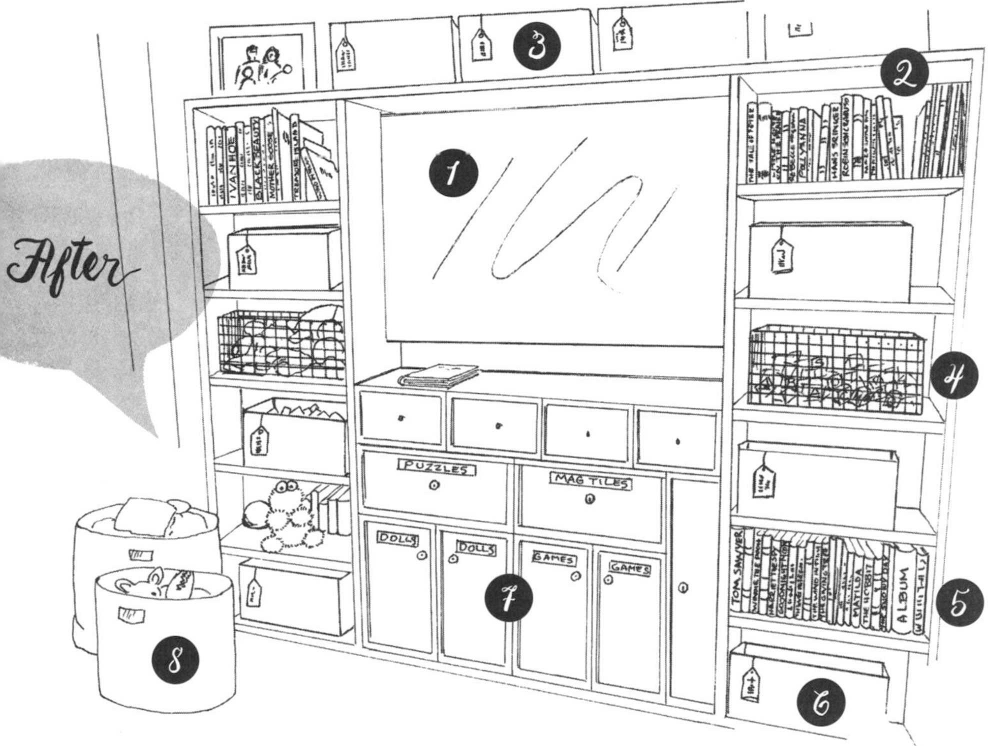

5 Store favorite books down low so kids can reach them on their own.

6 Labeled opaque bins are best for Classics and Funs, but down low like this, anyone can see what's in them—perfect for Organics and Smarts.

7 Cabinet doors are a boon to Classics and Funs. Labeling keeps them from becoming junk cabinets or a graveyard for unloved toys and games. Labels with photos? Even better.

8 These bins look much better in the playroom. Also, they're perfect for dress-up clothes and stuffed animals. Label and categorize. "Miscellaneous" bins make it hard for kids to find things.

If you have open shelving for toys in a playroom, buy opaque bins. Cabinets and closets are a great way to hide toy storage in mixed-use areas, but kids tend to forget stuff is in there, so it's up to you to rotate those toys in and out. Your dream scenario is a wall of closets with adjustable shelves inside. It's one step for kids to see everything and equally easy to hide the mess in one step. You'll be happier if toy storage in kids' bedrooms is separate from clothing, but space will dictate that. If you care where bins are placed, label shelves as well as bins.

PixieTip!

Narrow categories make it easier for kids to find things, and you'll take the time to maintain them. For example, keep dolls separate from doll clothes. The broader a category, the more likely the category will morph into "miscellaneous" over time.

Schedule "the purge"

Schedule an annual toy purge in your calendar. Precede this project by scheduling a time for your kids to pick out one toy they want to give to charity. Personally, we've found this sometimes tips them off that "the purge" is coming!

Another time to schedule a purge for kids' stuff is at the end of each semester. Go through their cubby, get rid of unimportant items, and transfer the artwork to a deep storage bin or a bin under the bed.

FUN FREEDOMS & FUN STRUCTURES

Kids' Rooms and Playroom Priorities for *Funs*

- Put the "fun" into cleanup.
- Coordinate your toy storage with bins to hide clutter, especially if it is in your general living space.
- Use narrow categories.
- Purge toys and artwork when inspired.

Make cleanup fun

You understand process and usually see kids' mess for what it is: temporary. This will be your saving grace in dealing with the chaos of organizing children and all their stuff. Unlike Classics, you know there's no sense in cleaning it up before they're done. The hardest part for you will be all the activities, school productions, and time issues these little buggers throw into the mix. We also suspect that most of you have contributed to the baby-wearing trend, so you don't have to treat them as separate people for a little while longer, or until your back starts to break.

We encourage all types to help their kids with cleaning up, and you guys excel at making it into a fun activity or game (e.g., "the one who can get all the Legos® back into their bins first gets a treat"). But, creative as you are, we're sure you can come up with something a lot more fun than that, of course.

Mix, match, and coordinate

You're okay mixing toy storage in a living area outside of a bedroom or playroom if it's practical and confined to one area of the room, but nobody enjoys stepping on Legos with their bare feet. Get some bins—existing ones that fit your décor, mixed in with new coordinating, opaque ones. You're good at remembering hidden items, so you'll know what is in opaque bins even without labels.

Narrow categories are best

Try sticking to narrow categories, such as keeping cars separate from trains. The broader you make a category—e.g., "transportation" for cars, trains, and planes—the more quickly the bin will become an unwieldy mess your kids won't play with.

Purge when inspired

To keep chaos at bay, purge the toys you know your kids never play with when the moment presents itself. The same goes for artwork and schoolwork. If you can involve them in some way, great! But because you'll do this activity when you're moved to do it, this might not be possible. However, if it's really important to you, have the kids pick out their least favorite toy to give to charity.

ORGANIC STRUCTURES & SMART STRUCTURES

Kids' Rooms and Playroom Priorities for *Organic/Smart Structures*

- Close the door on a playroom and bedrooms when you don't have the energy to clean.
- Make sure your bins match your décor if toys need to share space with living areas.
- Using big bins and big categories to organize the toys will help with maintenance.
- Put annual or biannual toy, artwork, and schoolwork purges in your calendar.
- Smart Structures: declutter annually—or have someone else do it.
- Organic Structures: digitize sentimental items, or farm it out to a service.

Close the door, or make sure your toy storage is adequate and matches your décor

Some people are baffled when you're annoyed by kids' toy clutter, because you can otherwise ignore a desk with piles of paper or a cluttered countertop. The difference is that your piles have purpose, while toy clutter doesn't. Though kids' messes are temporary, it's still really annoying for you to see them strewn about without rhyme or reason or a proper home—especially if the toys are in your living area or under your feet.

If space forces you to share your own living space with kids' toys, then make sure toys have proper homes in your living space, be they bins or shelves, where you can quickly pitch things and create order. Go the extra mile and make sure your toy storage is attractive and large enough, and matches the décor. Otherwise, the mismatched storage with toys poking out is going to bug you. If you're lucky and you've got a playroom, then the perfect temporary solution to a mess is to close the door. We know the mess will eventually bug you, even behind closed doors, and we also know that it feels a lot easier to take care of it later yourself than to get your kids involved. Do what's easiest.

Big bins, big categories

Go with transparent bins and open shelving when organizing kids' stuff. You don't need to have everything hidden away behind cabinet doors or in a closet to feel like these rooms are organized. Bigger bins and bigger categories are the way to go in these rooms. Steer clear of smaller bins for small categories—they're not likely to stay that way for long, and it's just an extra detail. This isn't the place to flex against your preferences, and you're better at the big picture: everything has to have a home.

Schedule the purge

As for purging, put it in your calendar as an annual To Do. If you do want the kids involved, schedule a time ahead of the purge to have them pick out toys they want to donate. Then, when they're not around, go to town. When it's too hard to make that call on your own and you want to avoid unwittingly getting rid of something precious, hide the donations for a month or two and see if they miss them. Schedule another annual or biannual purge for kids' artwork and schoolwork. Have two bins—one for schoolwork and one for artwork—so they don't get too full too fast. Smart Structures should consider farming this project out to a kids' digitizing service.

ORGANIC FREEDOMS & SMART FREEDOMS

Kids' Rooms and Playroom Priorities for *Organic/Smart Freedoms*

- Organize using larger categories than you want—you'll thank us later.
- Create order by using transparent bins, except in a formal living area.
- Purge when you can't stand the mess, you're planning a party, or a visit from someone judgmental is scheduled.
- Make sure bins are big enough for whatever you're storing in them.
- Plan kids' outfits ahead of time.
- Organic Freedoms: rely on Later Boxes to slowly go through keepsakes.

Use broad categories

You understand that kids' messes are temporary. They're annoying to see, but you'll get to it eventually. Hence, a playroom with a door you can close is ideal for you. An out-of-sight mess means it can be out of mind for as long as you prefer. But even you guys are eventually going to get disgusted with a big pile of toys in the middle of the playroom floor.

Regardless of whether a separate playroom is possible, when you get around to organizing kids' stuff, stick to big, broad categories. Since details are not your strength, sometimes you overthink labels and end up going overboard with hyper-detailed categories (like one client who had a separate bin for her daughter's Barbie doll shoes). Don't. It'll drive you mad trying to maintain it. Go ahead: mix doll clothes with dolls, cars with trains and tracks. The kids will find things, and you will not lose your mind trying to keep everything separate. Toy chests were invented for you guys. But that doesn't give you carte blanche to get all opaque bins or hide everything away.

Transparent bins are best, but not in a living room

Transparent bins are ideal for seeing and remembering what's inside, especially when toy storage is behind closet or cabinet doors. But if you're forced to share adult space with kids' toys in a multipurpose living area, then push your preferences and label attractive opaque bins that match your aesthetic. The utter lack of beauty that transparent bins create will annoy you.

Purge for parties

The best time to purge toys is when you're about to lose it if you see another stuffed animal, or if it's a disaster and someone judgmental is visiting you. The latter makes a great deadline. Katie often uses kids' birthday parties to take on this gargantuan task. In fact, right now as we write this, her three-year-old is about to turn four, and it's inspiring her to get the playroom in order for the party. (Naturally, after ten four-year-olds go to town on it, it will be a mess for months afterward.) Get rid of the toys as soon as you finish purging—put them in bags in your car—because if they linger or you store them somewhere else, you might forget about them for a while, and the kids might rediscover them and put them back into rotation . . . defeating the whole point of purging.

What to purge? Purge the toys you know your kids will never play with because they never do. If you happen to be able to involve them in some way, great, but you'll probably do this activity in a rush. It's not the end of the world, but if it's really important to you, every so often have the kids pick out their least favorite toy to give to charity.

Large is "in charge"

If you get a keepsake bin for your kids, make sure it's large—as in *really* large—because it'll take you longer than others to get around to going through it and purging every once in a while.

Plan kids' outfits weekly

If you're in charge of your kids' outfits, then consider creating a week (or more) of outfits when doing laundry, so there's less thinking to do when you're getting ready each day. Hanging sweater boxes can be the perfect place to put the prearranged outfits. When kids are big enough, they can get the outfits and dress themselves—unless they're the type to create their own outrageous outfits and you want more editorial control.

Thank God for Later Boxes

Especially if you're an Organic Freedom, you are going to need lots of these for all sorts of sentimental items.

Kids' Bedrooms & Playroom Checklist

- ☐ Donated or recycled any toys that are broken, unloved, or secretly hated by you (or put them in Later Boxes for especially sentimental children)
- ☐ Set up a large, secured floor-to-ceiling toy storage system that can grow with your child
- ☐ Purchased coordinating or matching bins for toys (more than you need!)
- ☐ Created labels for toy bins and baskets that combine visuals and words, especially if the children are young
- ☐ Purchased some form of short or double hang and shelves for kids' closets
- ☐ Bought matching, kid-size hangers
- ☐ Purchased storage bins for outgrown clothes, sentimental items, and kids' artwork and schoolwork
- ☐ Transferred outgrown clothing, sentimental items, and prized artwork and schoolwork to deep storage (or took pictures of them for a physical or digital album)

CHAPTER THIRTEEN

The Garage, Attic, and Storage Spaces

Remember the final scene from *Indiana Jones and the Raiders of the Lost Ark*, when they purposely store the super-dangerous Ark of the Covenant in a vast government storage facility in a closed, opaque box next to thousands of identical boxes *purposefully* lost to the millennia? That's how irretrievable things can get in garages, attics, basements, or self-storage units. Since most of you don't possess dangerous artifacts, and retrieval is the building block of organization, you're going to need a better storage system—or your prized possessions will be *accidentally* lost to the millennia. We call these places "deep storage" because you only need what's in them once a year, at best. Outside of luggage, anything used monthly, weekly, or daily shouldn't be in there.

UNIVERSAL SOLUTIONS

Garage, Attic, and Storage-Space Essentials for *All Types*

- Don't waste time trying to make this area perfect and pristine.
- Measure the space—including weird architectural details.
- Plan where items should go, with frequently used deep-storage items (e.g., luggage) in the most accessible area.
- Get a sturdy metal shelving system to prevent or limit stacking.
- Purchase matching transparent bins in one to three sizes, and label them.
- Be careful about where you store delicate items, as damp basements wreak havoc.
- Chuck or donate any practical items left untouched in two-plus years.
- Curate sentimental items.
- Promptly remove unwanted items from your living space, using closet "donation" bins or your car trunk if your storage space is difficult to access.

Don't obsess over this area

Deep storage is where seasonal items, vacation gear, and sentimental things spend their golden years, and where wanted (yet not all *that* wanted) possessions go to linger in purgatory. If you've been diligently organizing your home, we bet a few of you've punted stuff into the general organizational abyss of the garage, attic, or basement. Don't stress about reorganizing things properly in here; as long as you've got enough room, you know where things are, and you can retrieve them. Far better that the part of your home where you live daily is organized than the dark space you rarely see. However, we assume you're reading this because your storage area is full of crap you don't want or need anymore.

Plan ahead and measure everything

Most of us simply stack boxes and bins or put them on top of each other, but this is what creates the vast Area-51 storage facility and makes retrieving anything super-annoying. Even getting a suitcase can be an ordeal if they're all stacked on top of each other instead of on shelves. First, measure these spaces and all of their nooks and crannies twice before purchasing anything. Generally plan where things should go, based on how often you need to access them.

Get adequate, sturdy shelving

Purging isn't the first step to getting organized in here; it's ensuring that you have adequate structure to store and retrieve what will remain. You will *always* need more shelves than you think. *Always.*

For basements and garages, we favor the kind of open metal shelving you find in professional kitchens. It's sturdy, large, and affordable. For attics or walk-in storage closets, we often use the customizable Elfa ventilated shelving, which allows you to create structure even in awkward spaces. Not everything will fit on shelves, but having them will prevent getting something from storage from feeling like a deep-sea dive.

Invest in transparent bins and labels

Purchase enough transparent bins to fill all shelves, and a few extra for on the floor. Even if you live alone, transparent bins with lids and labels are essential to future retrieval, no matter what your personality type, because this is deep storage. Unless you have a photographic memory, you are going to lose track of stuff put in an opaque box. Avoid the growing "miscellaneous" stockpile by marking all bins with a label maker or a permanent marker and masking tape. Also make sure the bins fit on your shelves and that you have different sizes to accommodate different types of items. Having only big bins is not a good idea, because they can get so heavy that they're immovable. Limit stacks to two or three bins tall. Once you start stacking more on top, they become irretrievable.

Find logical homes for delicate items

Sentimental objects that can be damaged by weather don't belong in a flood-prone basement or an attic that hits 100 degrees every summer. Things that cannot safely be touched by water should be in water-tight transparent bins on wall-mounted shelves. Papers, photos, and precious clothing should be stored in archival cardboard boxes away from water *and* sunlight, unless you're hoping decay or fading will help you ditch them.

Purge, baby, purge

As always with the rest of your home, you need to go through everything in this space if you want to organize it. We might not be as strict as Japanese organizing guru Marie Kondo, but she has a point about essentially "touching" everything in your house to make sure it has a current purpose. Otherwise, what's the point in wasting time organizing this space?

Throw away/donate/sell anything practical you haven't used (or thought of!) in over two years, as well as anything that's broken, moldy, or infested with bugs or rodents (ugh, yes, we once found an old mouse nest during a basement organizing job). Let go of the same trivial reasons you have for keeping anything in any room, like how much you spent on something (it's a sunk cost at this point) or "It might come in handy" (everything *could* come in handy). In reality, maybe two things from an attic come in handy over a twenty-year period—excluding seasonal items or hand-me-downs—so you're essentially keeping a room full of junk for maybe the 1 percent that might actually be used again. Think about it.

PixieTip!

Trash bags full of junk are ubiquitous in storage spaces because they're on hand when you need to store stuff in a hurry. We are all guilty of doing it. The best way to avoid the "curbside collection" look in your garage or attic is to have empty bins on hand to take in new stuff at a moment's notice.

If you're in an apartment and don't have the luxury of an attic or basement, then get a climate-controlled storage unit. Sometimes realizing that you're actually paying rent for stuff you don't want in your daily life is just the inspiration to start throwing it away.

Regarding old computers that have stuff you might need on them, have a service shop download it onto a hard drive or CD, *label* what's on that drive or disk, wipe the machine clean, and call it a day. Recycle old electronics or appliances, or sell them if they're newer. If you're keeping a laptop computer (slightly less space-hogging than a desktop computer), attach a power cord to it, and then label what's on it and why you've kept it (sometimes you forget).

Things to ditch without worry include old picture frames you no longer use, obsolete cell-phone chargers, obsolete cable/computer wires, any wire with a purpose you don't know, and old sheets or blankets that don't make the linen-closet cut.

Pixie Tip!

Those clear vacuum suction storage bags that "create space" are a waste of time and money. Purge before you even contemplate buying those disasters. They make retrieving things impossible—you have to re-inflate them to get one item. They wrinkle everything and stack horribly. They're essentially overpriced, clear-plastic garbage bags.

If it feels like you have an entire house to go through, it's easy to get overwhelmed. But 1-800-GOT-JUNK offers one of the best services. After you cherry-pick, they remove everything else and find homes for it all, reselling and donating what they can. The service costs money, but it's totally worth it when tackling a massive decluttering project.

Curate mementos

Of course, sitting around in these areas there's more than random junk that needs to be addressed. You also need to get tough about beloved items like baby clothes, a departed loved one's furniture, and other mementos from your past. Curate your sentimental items by picking the most meaningful and/or highest quality. For each item, ask yourself: "Is it iconic?"; "Will it stand the test of time?"; "Is it a unique artifact or antique that I will 100 percent use someday?"; and "Is it something someone would remotely appreciate receiving one day?" If the answer is "yes" to any of those four questions, keep 'em—especially if you have the room.

For instance, Kelly keeps cards from her husband until it's time for deep storage, then chucks cards where he just signed his name. Personal correspondence may be fascinating, but when you're dead and gone, what grandkid is going to treasure store-bought greeting cards with throw-away sentiments on them?

All baby clothes beyond hand-me-down stage are full of precious memories to you, but the most precious items—special dresses, iconic T-shirts, baptismal gowns, etc.—are the only ones someone would want to receive one day. Clothing items that don't last include those made with stretchy material—ahem, socks—and those with elastic waistbands.

If something doesn't make the cut with the four questions, but you still can't bear the idea of things going to a dumpster or leaving the family, talk to someone who does estate sales in your area, or ask if other family members are interested. E-mail a photograph of the item, along with dimensions, to limit the time spent communicating about it.

PixieTip!

Parents with grown kids: at some point you have to let go of their stuff, and you might as well use the opportunity to entice more visits from them and their other halves. Give them enough advance warning to come by and retrieve it. If they ignore your warning, ask them if they'd rather you threw everything out, shipped it in boxes, or set up a moving van to get it to them. Let go of the past so you can start making new memories with your loved ones.

Remove junk from your premises

Outside of contacting estate-sales people when you're overwhelmed, you may have noticed that we haven't discussed selling items. It's not an accidental omission. Donating goods and then throwing out what's clearly trash (or recycling) is the easiest solution. Selling just one item online, on the other hand, can take a long time and a lot of extra work (e.g., pricing, tagging, photos, listing, shipping). It's almost not worth the money. We're not saying it can't be done, but it takes a specific type of person to see it through. For many people, the To Dos involved are daunting, tedious tasks that postpone the act of organizing. If you've got a week and think you can get it done, go for it. If not, wipe the slate clean right now: the city dump, 1-800-GOT-JUNK, DonateStuff®, or Goodwill.

Garage

1 Pegboards are old-school organization, and while some Classics can take them on, there are newer and easier ways to store gardening gear. This pegboard isn't working.

2 You have to move a bucket of mulch to get to the gardening tools? Too hard!

3 The croquet set is in danger of falling on someone's head.

4 Kids are going to need help getting their favorite riding toy out.

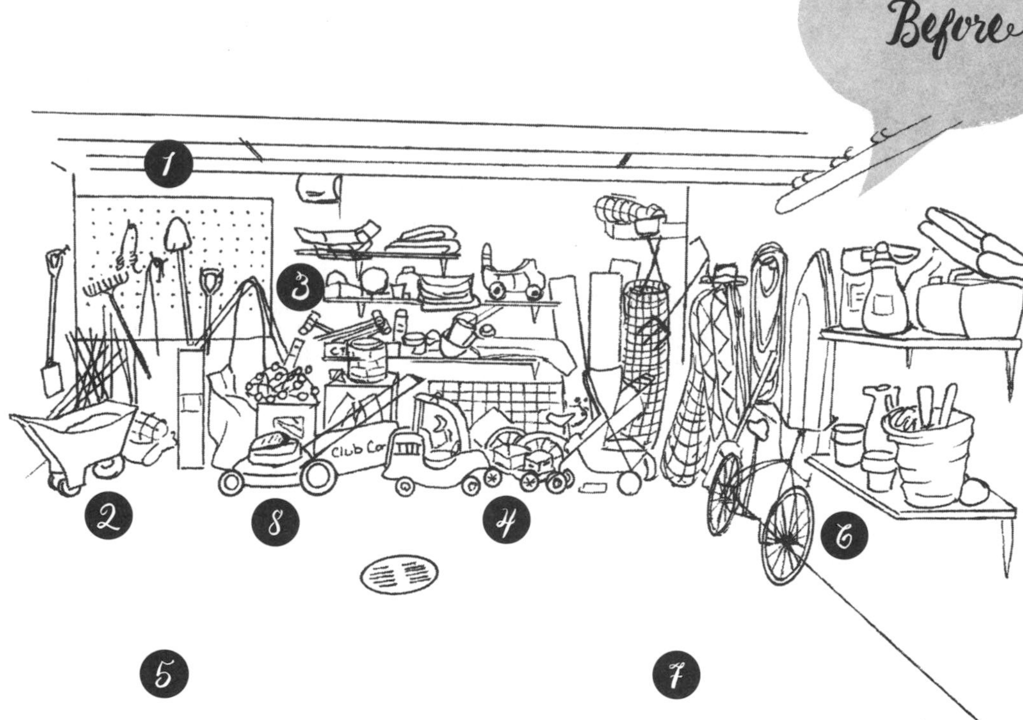

5 What's in here? We can't tell. . . . Can you?

6 These ill-placed bicycle and shelves make getting out of the car impossible for passengers.

7 One could argue that all this open space for two cars means this garage is organized. To some degree, it is, but can you find everything easily and in one step? Not so much.

8 The only thing that's easy to retrieve is the lawn mower.

1 Wait—there was a ladder in here? Is there anything well-placed hooks can't do?

2 Gardening tools work well when hung all in a row on a specially designed strip.

3 The croquet set now has a shelf space all its own.

4 Yes, you can also avail yourself of matching bins in the garage. Make sure they have labels unless you live alone.

5 Sleds! *That's* where they were. The kids can even hang them back up neatly.

6 There was a garden hose in here? Again, a simple strip of wall hooks can work wonders.

7 The riding toys are positioned face-first, like parked cars. This way the kids can get them out by themselves, and you can get something else done!

8 Notice the bicycle on the wall with special bike hooks. It's toward the back, so everyone can get out of the car.

CLASSIC FREEDOMS & CLASSIC STRUCTURES

Garage, Attic, and Storage-Space Priorities for *Classics*

- Put "organize storage" on your written To-Do list.
- No argument on labels!
- Transparent bins are a must.
- Keep a running inventory of items in here.
- Classic Freedoms: if you have trouble parting with things, create space for Later Boxes.

Make it a priority

Ignore our "universal advice" about not obsessing over messy deep storage; if your attic, basement, or garage is not organized, it will bug you in some deep corner of your mind. The inner peace you'll have every time you climb into your perfectly organized attic to get the holiday decorations is almost immeasurable. Even if you can't get to it for two or three months, or even a year, put "organize deep storage" in your calendar, along with the chore of purchasing bins and shelves ahead of time. This act alone will make you feel better about the state of your storage area.

PixieTip!

If your storage space is hard to reach (e.g., a pull-down attic or off-site unit), keep donation/storage bins in a closet or even a car trunk until you can get to it. This way, you've at least removed these items from your daily existence and made space for other important stuff.

Labels are mandatory in here

We've had many Classic clients who don't use labels in their house because they and their families know where things go. Great. Storage is different: don't ignore us on this one. Label shelves and boxes so people don't mess up your system because—believe us—they will. But if you've got a label to point to, you can politely ask why they heck they put Easter stuff in the "Xmas" box.

Ditto for transparent bins

While you might abhor transparent bins out in the open of your living areas, don't go with your instinct to hide mess behind opaqueness in storage areas. Put aside your thrifty nature and purchase a bunch of matching see-through bins. This is one area in your home where you can always close the door on a contained "mess."

> *PixieTip!*
>
> Oh, and please fight any urge to keep your empty appliance boxes. There's no prize for the klutz who still has the box their Mr. Coffee® came in, and Ms. Martha herself would never keep hers around. Keeping it for a move? Instead, hire some decent movers to pack the coffeemaker for you—or carefully pack it yourself, as assiduity is one of your fortes—but don't waste precious real estate on empty boxes.

Be a nerd and inventory this room

An extra step that we perform for clients is to make an inventory of what's in their storage area. Try to create one on your mobile device as you are putting things into transparent bins and onto shelves. With a digital inventory, you can easily add to or subtract as things come and go. It can be a big, generic list of what's in storage, perhaps with a note next to each item about where it's stored; or you can get crazy and list by category or by bin. Print it out and put it in a file for everyone to find. We've never met anyone who keeps a perfect inventory because, when you're in a hurry taking things in and out, you don't always have the time to write it down. But the very fact that it exists will make you a storage rock star.

Classic Freedoms have an Achilles heel

Classic Freedoms can throw away many less-important items as time separates the wheat from the chaff; but, being more sentimental about objects, they tend to store more things than Classic Structures. For example, after ten years a Classic Freedom friend finally decided to get rid of her beloved grandparents' tattered, ugly upholstered headboard, but was overcome with sadness when the trash haulers took it away. If you find that parting with sentimental items cuts to the bone, create an area for future Later Boxes in this area.

FUN FREEDOMS & FUN STRUCTURES

Garage, Attic, and Storage-Space Priorities for Funs

- Scour your brain to find a way to make organizing this room fun.
- Yes, label.
- Get colored transparent bins if you can.
- Fun freedoms: if you must, get morbid while you purge.

The toughest job in the world is motivating yourself to clean out your garage

Organizing deep storage will be bottom-of-the-list for most Funs. Isn't there some kind of film festival, or county fair, or *anything else* more fun happening right now? Yes. But you have to get to it at some point. Most junk is the physical manifestation of procrastination, and it will keep accumulating like snow in the mountains: if you don't shovel after you get a few inches, beware, because the snow keeps on coming . . . forever.

Throwing a soiree may inspire you to tidy up your living spaces, but it's harder to create a forced deadline to clean up the mishmash of boxes in the attic or basement. Nobody wants to party in your garage or attic . . . or do they? We know one family that gives an annual garage cleanout as a Mother's Day gift. It's a brilliant trick, as it's a gift (can't beg out of it) and a deadline but also a social activity, which makes it *almost* fun. Anything in this vein that makes this project even *slightly* appealing will work.

Other than creating a party around a purge, the best way for you to take care of any chore is to do it in the moment when you're disgusted with the mess and have the energy to tackle the task. Perhaps the next time you're looking for that Honest Abe costume for a fancy dress party might be the time to finally get your deep storage in order, *unless* it's only an hour before you have to go. When you're putting the costume away after the party, take stock of what's taking up so much space in your storage area, and start by purging that stuff.

Pixie Tip!

Always overestimate the time it will take you to tackle a project—by a lot (just a gentle reminder that you don't have the best internal clock)..

You can also finish this project with an inventory of what's in there. Jotting a note down on your phone is handy, even if you don't keep it up-to-date.

Transparent bins and labels are key

Even something as mundane as getting different-colored transparent boxes to help you distinguish between different storage items can lend a modicum of *joie de vivre*. Not to beat a dead horse with labels, but you need them even if you go the color-coded bin route. They will help you remember if green is for Christmas or St. Patrick's Day.

Don't draw out good-byes

Among Funs, Fun Freedoms have the tougher time letting go of sentimental items. One trick to letting go is to ask yourself whether it's something someone else would keep after you died. Do the same when revisiting Later Boxes. It's tempting to postpone the decision again, but you're better off ripping off the Band-Aid® today when you're already dealing with this mess.

Appeal to your practical nature to get rid of empty appliance boxes as well. They are an insane waste of square footage and a spot where rodents and bugs love to burrow. You guys will take the time to protect fragile items for a move; so unless you plan to sell a used coffeemaker a few years hence and need the extra dollar it fetches because it comes with original packing material, dump these items.

ORGANIC STRUCTURES & SMART STRUCTURES

Garage, Attic, and Storage-Space Priorities for *Organic/Smart Structures*

- Put "organize storage" on your To-Do list when this area starts to cause you stress.
- Abstain from using existing boxes, unless they're transparent with tops.
- Organic Structures: go through Later Boxes on a regular basis.

Prioritize this brutal task when you can't take it anymore

You'll know it's time to put this task on your To-Do list when the irretrievable state of things in there makes fetching seasonal items exhausting.

Do it right

As much as we try to take personality type into account, truthfully there is not a lot of wiggle room for organizing deep storage. You usually have an instinct toward organization, especially when starting out; but eventually storage areas become a hodgepodge of stacked boxes with a patchwork of stories behind them because you used whatever you had on hand at the time or were able to quickly pick up at the store—and because you keep more clutter than almost half the population.

Harness your big-picture planning skills and take the time to do it right—in whatever order you see fit. Buy new transparent bins, shelves that truly fit the space, and labels for specifying what's inside the bins. Labeling gives you a better chance of keeping storage organized longer, but use big category labels—"Christmas!"—unless you have too much stuff and need to delineate a category within a box (e.g., "Kids' Clothes" by child or size). Avoid "Miscellaneous" bins. If you spend the extra time to label, a storage inventory list isn't necessary, as long as everything is visible and easy to reach.

Saying good-bye is the hardest part

Organic Structures: deep storage is where you should put all those Later Boxes we recommended in earlier chapters, and some of you may have a *ton* of them. In this scenario, unless storage space is a pressing issue going forward, keep them all in the same area. Once a year, put "Go through a Later Box (or two!)" and "Donate/sell contents of Later Box" on your To-Do list. Put whatever survives—what you remember is in each box (and want) before opening it—in a proper bin, and label it. Do your best to get as much donated or sold as possible. In time, you will winnow down this space to only transparent bins full of true gems.

Smart Structures: you're decent curators of riffraff when you're determined to get rid of things. Even still, we know you'll be loath to throw away a few items. Therefore, check in every once in a while to make sure you still feel that way about these physical reflections of your achievements in deep storage (your children will just take them to the dump or use them as kindling after you have shuffled off this mortal coil, anyway). Also, keep in mind that deep storage is a perfect organizing task to delegate once you've purged things and selected the categories you want to maintain going forward.

ORGANIC FREEDOMS & SMART FREEDOMS

Garage, Attic, and Storage-Space Priorities for *Organic/Smart Freedoms*

- Don't freak out about these areas.
- Break this project down into bite-size pieces, and hire help if possible.
- Measure, measure, measure!
- You can do without transparent bins . . . as long as you label.

Take a deep breath

It's an understatement to say that these spaces overwhelm you when left unattended for periods of time (which they often are). Our Organic Freedom grandmother used to jokingly worry that her attic was going to collapse from the weight of what was up there. Your storage area is rarely ever going to look Pinterest-enviable; but honestly, who cares? You've got more important organizational fish to fry. Don't stress about reorganizing things properly as long as you've got some room in deep storage, can retrieve things without injuring yourself, and *sort of* know where things are. If this isn't the case—you keep buying new stuff, not remembering/realizing that you already had five beach chairs stored away—heed our advice below.

Bite-size makes it palatable

Don't make it into one massive project. Break it down into four bite-size pieces—plan, buy, purge, label—and for goodness's sake, hire someone to help you along the way, because there's so much decision-making involved that you shouldn't do this task alone. It doesn't have to be an organizer, but it's important that whoever you hire helps you physically get things out of your house. You can enlist a spouse's or a roommate's help, but just remember that you run the risk of making this task a much more conflict-prone project when you do it together.

> **PixieTip!**
>
> You're not the personality types who should personally sell a plethora of items—it often ends up unfinished if you have no help and no deadline.
>
> If there's only energy or money to do one thing in here? Purge. If other personality types' clutter buildup is like snow accumulation in the Great Lakes, then yours is like the Arctic Circle. You've got to shovel, or you'll be buried alive.

Measure, then plan

Measuring is a detailed and specific task—not your forte—and therefore it's important to sweat the details and triple-check your measurements (or have someone else do it) before you shop. Then let your mind wander to come up with a plan about how to set things up and arrange them to improve access. Next, buy shelving and new bins. If these purchases remain unused alongside the mess in your storage area for a while, don't beat yourself up.

Opaque is okay, as long as you label

Label each box with what's inside in broad terms—e.g., "Kids' Clothes." But having multiple bins within a category requires more details. Sure, you can see what's inside translucent bins, but can you really determine that it's a toddler "size 2" clothing and not "size 3"? For opaque boxes, label the tops and at least one side with masking tape and/or a Sharpie®. The next time you're inspired, put together the shelves, hire a handyman, or heck, you can even hire someone from TaskRabbit® or Craigslist® to do it for you. It's not brain surgery; it's just time-consuming and boring.

Garage, Attic, and Storage-Space Checklist

- ☐ Measured storage space
- ☐ Planned out the storage system, with more frequently used items in more accessible areas
- ☐ Bought strong metal shelving that fits the space
- ☐ Purchased translucent matching bins and labels
- ☐ Purchased archival boxes for precious paper or clothing
- ☐ Purged practical items left untouched for two-plus years
- ☐ Went through all sentimental items to determine which are the most valuable
- ☐ Removed items to be donated, trashed, recycled, or sold from living and storage areas

PART III

KEEPING THE PEACE

After years of working with cohabiting couples, as well as each other, we've learned a thing or two about the challenges different PixieTypes face when they're forced to share one space. It ain't easy; but along with a little love, a lot of understanding, and some serious acceptance and compromise, our advice can help you out of some major scrapes. Good luck and godspeed!

CHAPTER FOURTEEN

You're driving me crazy! (compromises for different PixieTypes)

It's easy to *say* "To each his own," but it's quite another thing to share a bed or a house with someone who leaves their wet towel on the floor of the bathroom (or—shudder—on the bed) after they shower *despite* the fact that you complain about it ad nauseam. Through our work, we've discovered that there are predictable organizational clashes that various cohabiting PixieTypes have. In this chapter, we summarize each PixieType's list of annoyances (which are by no means comprehensive) with other types and offer solutions for keeping the peace. In the case above, the guilty towel person is likely an Organic Freedom or a Smart Freedom and doesn't have an easy place to hang their towel. Mount a couple of towel hooks, explain their use to the towel bandit, and voilà! Another marriage saved. (We probably missed our calling as marriage counselors. . . .)

UNIVERSAL SOLUTIONS

Compromise Essentials for *All Types*

- Communicate your organizational standards by room (verbally or on paper).
- Be open to compromise, but know your limits and pick your battles.
- Explain your organizational systems once they're in place.
- Get others' input on those systems and change 'em up when they're not working.
- Communicate before throwing things out.
- Remember: it's not personal, it's personality!

Agree to ground rules for what constitutes organized and tidy

Ground rules are basic agreements or compromises on how different areas of the house should look and operate. These kinds of compromises are rarely straightforward, which is why communication beforehand can be so helpful. At the very least, the next time you find your Organic Freedom beloved's coat on the dining-room table, try to communicate on the fly before you go postal. A Classic Structure wants dirty clothes to always go in hampers and to have no clothing draped on furniture. An Organic Freedom thinks as long as the clothes aren't on the floor, it's good. A compromise between these polar-opposite types might be to agree to remove the hamper lids and mount some hooks so the Organic Freedom can drape clothes on hooks instead of the chair.

For example: What's your definition of a clean kitchen? A Fun or Classic might define a clean kitchen as having empty countertops and an empty sink at almost all times. But this would be too much for a tidy Smart Structure or Organic Structure. A logical compromise might be maintaining clean countertops and always running the dishwasher before bed, even if that means there are dirty dishes in the sink at times. We can already imagine a few Funs and Classics bristling at this lax ground rule. And there's the rub—you can have your spotless kitchen, but if there isn't universal buy-in, you'll be the one doing it.

Communicate your organizational system and get input

In the real world, tons of people will never in a million years sit down and go over their organizational expectations room by room with each other—Kelly's husband's eyes visibly glazed over when she suggested this idea—which brings us to Plan B, or "communication on the fly without attitude." The latter is tougher than you'd think, because you're likely to do on-the-fly organizational communication when someone is irritating you. Try not to do Plan B during these moments. Instead, do it when you create a new system or notice that nobody's been following your system.

Anyway, once you've spent a lot of time creating a new organizational system, don't expect everyone to know how it's supposed to run. Communicate with everyone in the household like you're giving an office tour to the new guy. Go over every detail. Believe it or not, it isn't always self-evident that yogurts are stored in the bin on the fridge door. These are the moments when you can elicit other people's input, something that needs to happen for any system to work. We get our clients' input for just this reason. If something still isn't working after a few office "tours," change it up. *It's easier to change a system than to change people's behavior.*

Pay attention to how someone disregards your system

If someone isn't putting clothing items or mail/papers where they should be, chances are their designated home is an ill-conceived spot. Before you do anything—including verbally unloading your annoyance on the person/people ignoring your method of organization—start by innocently asking them why the system isn't working for them. Put the onus on yourself and your system's failure to function as a way to get them to be less defensive about their contribution to the mess. Chances are that, from this conversation, you'll come up with a tweak that will help it work better. Maybe the closet or mailboxes are overstuffed, or maybe the designated homes are not logical or too far from where the pertinent people naturally unload when they get home. Maybe you need to reconfigure where their mail inbox goes.

Pick your battles

Revisit your ground rules and systems (whether written or mental) with each other in a year and see what solutions you can develop for the presumably growing list of pet peeves and tweaks for the organizational solutions that are not working. Because, of course, there are times when even one-step wonder hooks or lidless hampers don't solve the problem, and that's when we remind readers of the age-old saying, *pick your battles*.

If you've had this conversation and determined that your system is A-OK, you've probably got an insanely stubborn person on your hands. It happens, and that means you're going to have to dig deep and find the compromise that irritates you the least. This is when our pick-your-battles advice comes to the fore. One Classic client could neither get her husband to stop buying bulk paper products and Costco-size toiletries that were impossibly big to use daily, nor get him to limit purchases to their available storage space. The compromise was that he can still go to Costco *as long as* he finds hidden homes for these items. Our client decided logical homes weren't as important as having them hidden, because seeing paper towels on her countertop irritated her. Also, he must transfer the contents of these massive bargain bottles to smaller, more user-friendly bottles when refills are necessary.

Communicate before throwing things out

Something that we can all forget to do in our zeal to get organized is telling people we're organizing and moving their things or (worse) throwing them out. There are items in your home that you might regard as joint property, or even your own property, that you freely throw out, not realizing that doing so will upset someone living with you. It doesn't mean you

> **PixieTip!**
>
> The "why" behind organizational pet peeves doesn't have to be complex. It can be as simple as "It annoys me."

can't get rid of these items. If you relay your intentions and put the items in a donation bin—a holding bin of sorts—and leave them there for a while before throwing them out, you'll have fewer fights. Case in point: Kelly just relearned this lesson when throwing away old, ugly, unused coffee mugs to make way for new matching mugs her husband had bought her for Christmas. Frankly, the betrayal he felt when he learned his mugs were gone might have been less if she'd brought home a boyfriend.

It's not personal

Whatever the organizational conflict is, remember that it's not personal, nor is it on purpose. Your brains are either wired differently, you had different upbringings, or both. This little kernel is often the only way some of us can pick up a towel that's on the floor or bed, day in and day out, and not erupt like Mount Vesuvius the next time we see the towel bandit drop a soaking towel on our bed. If that isn't enough to calm you down, then get drastic. For example, if said towel bandit were dead, you'd find yourself in a puddle of tears or verklempt (if crying isn't your thing) when you first realized you'll never have to pick up towels from the floor or your bed anymore. Death has a way of making us realize that, even though organization is essential to an easier life, it's not the most important thing. It's tough to follow through on this advice, but it's good to remember. And on that cheerful note, let's dig into some organizational clashes by type!

CLASSICS

You have pet peeves with everyone because your organizational requirements are the most extensive and demanding. Yeah, that's code for: you're the number-one complainers. Your biggest clashes are with Organics and Smarts because they miss the important details of your organizational rules, which can be considered minor or trivial to others. Regardless of who you are dealing with, designated homes for things need to be spelled out and specific: coats go on hooks or on hangers, never on chairs; shoes go by the shoe bench.

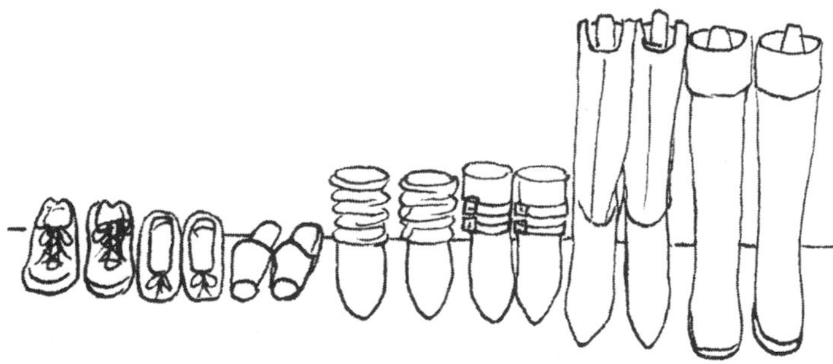

Problems with Other Classics

- You have slight—yet important—variations of cluttered or clean.
- You have different ideas about what constitutes a proper home for things.

While it may seem unusual or unexpected that you'd have organizational problems with fellow Classics, it's not. You're alike, which is not the same thing as being clones. You are amazing rule followers, especially when it's reciprocal—i.e., your voice and your opinions are both heard. Your conflicts with Classics are easily solved with communication. If you implement our universal advice on the previous pages and lay out your organizational expectations ahead of time, most involve very minor, yet important, compromises. We give this advice to everybody, but you guys are probably the only ones who'll actually do it.

Problems with Funs

- They have different definitions of being on time.
- They are less tidy.
- They are hard to pin down for advance plans and may procrastinate.

You're almost as copacetic with Funs as you are with fellow Classics, because they share so many of your organizational principles—with one main exception: their seeming inability to be consistently on time for social functions. It's tough, but not impossible, for them to do. Once you've identified the Funs in your life and have confirmed that this trait drives you crazy, feel free to lie to them about the start time of events. Sometimes they will catch on, but if you're clever about it—only doing so when it really matters to you, or pretend you got the times wrong if they discover—they'll be none the wiser. If this seems disingenuous, it is, and you're nicer than we are.

Funs can also be messy when organizing areas that aren't their passion—paper and mail are frequently the culprits. Create rules for them about where paper must go: for example, if you have a cubby system. If this doesn't work—mail overflows in their bin or items are lost—place their mail in their daily bag along with roving office supplies so they can go through it at their leisure and it's out of your sight. Communication on the go works best with Funs, so explain your organizing systems or Dos and Don'ts, whatever they may be. You'll likely never get them to sit down and come up with a list of their organizational Dos and Don'ts, but they'll generally follow what you create.

Finally, when a Fun seems disorganized or messy, chances are they need a deadline to get their act in gear. We all procrastinate, but they're just a little bit better at it when it's something they loathe. As for getting a Fun to commit when you're planning an event, we have one Fun Structure client who might have two or three options of what to do with his evening—business-related events or networking—and he chooses which to attend that day or week, depending on his mood. This is a hard type of person to pin down; but if it's a loved one and you need to be sure they'll come, make sure they know how important it is to you. They're not monsters, they're just not inclined to do boring things unless it's an absolute must. When it's the latter, they're there with bells on.

Problems with Organic Structures & Smart Structures

- They miss important details vis-à-vis tidying and cleaning.
- They have different definitions of clutter.
- They leave cupboard doors open.
- They hold on to more stuff.

You're on the same page with Organic Structures and Smart Structures when it comes to planning and getting things done, but you part ways when it comes to details of tidying and cleaning, not to mention clutter. The problem with cleaning is that they are not bothered by the details of mess as quickly as you are. A kitchen can be left a little untidy for longer before it bugs them; or piles on a surface can go unnoticed for a while. A detail like dusting is something that might go missed by them until it's very obvious, whereas you'd notice it much earlier and be annoyed. Unlike some other types, they know you should dust and get the benefit behind the efforts; they just don't prioritize the finer details as much as you do. You can try to communicate your organizational likes and dislikes to them and they'll do the same, but chances are that yours will be more exacting than theirs. Often, to get your home to your own standards, the onus will fall upon you unless you find basic broad compromises that work for both of you. Too many rules, and they might ignore you altogether.

They're not as bothered by visual clutter as you and they need things out to remember them, so finding compromises to clutter is tough. The compromise solutions that tend to work are ones that have structure and are contained but are also *visible*. When a compromise isn't possible, the person most in charge of maintaining the household has to win out, because it's their brain wiring that's running it; so for things to function best, the systems need to fit how they think.

Not all Organic and Smart Structures leave cupboard doors or closet doors open, but many do, and it's a great mystery to Classics who take these detailed actions for granted. Knowing that a client does this is an immediate flag as to who we are dealing with. They're also a bit more relaxed about time than you are. Most Organic Structures run about five minutes behind because they're always trying to get one more thing done from their To-Do list; but if you let them know how this upsets you, they'll never do it again. Smart Structures usually run about ten minutes behind, because usually whatever they're doing on their To-Do list is more important to them than anything else. But if being late is really upsetting you, describing to them how it affects you will help them get better about it.

Organic and Smart Structures also tend to have more stuff than you, notwithstanding Classics who hoard pantry items. In general, Organic Structures have trouble letting go of things, for a variety of reasons. Usually they don't want the things to go into a landfill, or there is a memory attached to the items. Smart Structures usually just have more stuff, because they're too busy with more important matters to regularly weed things out. Plus they collect trophies of their accomplishments along the way, be it the books they've read or professional career markers like investment banker tombstones.

Organic Structures and Smart Structures are not hopeless and can definitely get rid of things when motivated—but not to the extent you'd prefer. So our main advice with clutter is to push your roomie as far as he or she can go *vis-à-vis* getting clutter out the door, then see what you can get them to put in storage. The latter will be your pathway to a living area free of clutter. Don't fight storage. Embrace it as a compromise that makes you guys live and work well together. You can revisit storage in a couple of years, and chances are they'll let go of more stuff. Organic Structures often just need time to let go. Smart Structures are trickier, because unless you've got some sound logic to get them to reconsider, they won't be willing to part with their stuff until they're six feet under.

Problems with Organic Freedoms & Smart Freedoms

- They have different definitions of being on time.
- They have very different notions about what constitutes tidy and clean.
- They are last-minute planners who often procrastinate.
- They have more clutter than you prefer.
- They leave cupboard doors open.

We're not sure how Classics live with Organic Freedoms and Smart Freedoms, because they are your organizational opposites; living with one of them can drive you crazy even if you love 'em. Their idea of a made bed is still your idea of messy; they leave clothes strewn around; they leave kitchen cupboard doors open; some even leave fridge doors open. They don't do dishes remotely when you think they should be done; they don't really consider being five or ten minutes late as *late*; they don't make advance plans; they try to change plans on you at the last minute; they need deadlines to accomplish tasks; they procrastinate; they accumulate clutter; some even write important To Dos on their hands (yes, we mean adults). After reading those descriptions, we know you've immediately thought of at least one person in your life who fits this bill. It's helpful to understand that these are not character flaws but personality traits. Love conquers all: it's the magic ingredient that makes these relationships work.

Once you've identified the Organic Freedoms or Smart Freedoms in your life and have confirmed that their being late drives you crazy, you can use the same tactics you use with Funs to get them to the church on time by lying to them about the start time of events.

As for different definitions of "tidy" and "clean," you need to get down to the basics with these cohabitants. Let them know your bare minimum expectations per room from the start, or you'll regret it. Organic Freedoms are often very sweet and will work hard to do the organizational tasks that you require, just to please you. You can get into the weeds of detailed organizing on a case-by-case basis later. But you must pick your battles, because your brains are very different. The clutter they accumulate that drives you mad just doesn't bug them. Okay, maybe a little. But they're a lot like Organic and Smart Structures and aren't bothered by all their stuff. You can help them declutter, but you're also going to have to accept a little more baggage than you might have on your own.

These folks can plan ahead and often do, but sometimes they forget these plans because they don't tend to write them down or refer to plans they have written down. They also are totally fine with changing plans last minute, which can be a big annoyance for you. But when there's nothing you can do about it, try removing yourself from their presence for a few moments. Otherwise, you'll just want to rip off their heads. Then come up with a new plan based on the annoying changes. Going forward, tell them you're not redoing your plans based on their whim every time. This goes down better right when you've acquiesced. The next time it happens—oh, there will be a next time—remind them that you warned them. Also keep in mind that stuff happens. Sometimes plans have to change. It's not *always* their fault.

FUNS

You're pretty flexible about who you live with, because your lack of rigidity regarding time means you can find common ground with Organic Freedoms and Smart Freedoms—what's five to thirty minutes late for a social function among friends?—while your attention to detail and ability to follow a pre-existing organizational system means you can handle living with the more organizationally demanding Classics, even with their borderline fascist feelings about time. Scheduling is the main area where you have organizational conflicts with other types.

Problems with Classics

- Their focus on being on time or early gets old.
- Their rigidity about planning and timing gets equally old.
- They are To-Do list aficionados who preach the benefits.

You appreciate living with Classics because most take it upon themselves to set up organizing systems for you to follow. They do the boring part; you benefit. Naturally, you have your opinions on organizing, especially if it involves a passion of yours—whether it's outdoor sports equipment or cooking paraphernalia. Speak up about how you like these areas to be set up, do it yourself, or forever hold your peace. Some Classics can overstep and get a bit carried away with organizing and household rules.

Timing and planning are the two areas where you have the most conflict with Classics. Time and schedules are not something set in stone in your world. You'll get to tasks when you want to, or when it makes the most sense. But Classics have their own timelines and don't feel relief until something's done. They're constantly ticking something off on a written To-Do list. Yours is in your head, but since they don't see it, you make them nervous. Sometimes these timelines make sense, and sometimes they're arbitrary. It's the latter that irk you if they don't fit into how and when you want to schedule something or accomplish a task.

For example, you appreciate a clean kitchen with the best of them, but you're not going to create one in the middle of a party when you and your friends are having an awesome time. Yes, we have a Classic friend who does this. You might do it in the middle of a party if, say, your in-laws are over and boring you to tears. The key for you to understand is that Classics detest the unknown. They're thinking: "Will the kitchen get done, or will I have to do it after the party?" By all means, do things on your timeline, but let Classics know *when* you plan to do something, and they'll back down.

Another conflict area is about being on time. This is a tough one because Classics never relent about it—they see it as being disrespectful when someone is late—and you'll never be 100 percent on time. When they go out of their way to ensure that you will be there at the appointed hour of their choosing, those are the times to make the effort and set an alarm. Other times, they'll gripe, but it won't be a big deal. You might also ask your Classic how important it is to them that you're on time, but you may not get a straight answer.

Now on to making plans. Many Classics set up plans way in advance, sometimes months. Obviously, for work-related things, or weddings, or reunions, you understand; but not for average weekend social plans. You'll gladly make advance plans when it's something you're excited about doing. You're only reticent to be tied down to a plan one to three months from now when it's an obligation or something you're not jazzed about. Don't put off Classics, as this will lead to a blowup sooner or later. Be up front that you're not excited to attend this event, but you will know by a certain, specified date and time. Like the above solution, you're giving Classics a little certainty by telling them *when* you're going to get back to them. These are practical people who can accept when something doesn't work out, but limbo is not a state they can stand for very long.

Finally, if you don't maintain a To-Do list and occasionally forget to do something, the Classic in your life is going to think you need a To-Do list. If you find these are helpful, go for it. If not, don't bother. Tell them you do have a To-Do list: "It's in my head; and for important things, I set an alarm on my phone." Then remind them that even people with To-Do lists forget things. If you feel like having a fight, cite a time *they* forgot something. But if you want to enjoy the rest of your day, leave that bit out. To-Do lists are not as foolproof as Classics think; they just give the illusion of control.

Problems with fellow Funs

- What you keep clean, tidy, or organized differs.

When something means a lot to you, you'll take the time to do it right. Funs keep the things they're most passionate about the most organized, and the rest falls to the wayside. Your main organizing beef with other Funs is that you don't always agree on what needs to be well organized. If you love to cook, then you're likely to keep (and insist upon) a tidy kitchen. You're a big reader? Your bookshelves look great and are well organized, but probably not vice versa for your kitchen if cooking isn't a love of yours. Obviously, there might be other reasons behind your organizational differences—different parents, upbringings, or cultures—but the best thing to do when living with another Fun, and you have these dichotomies, is to divide and conquer. Your ground rules rule the day where your passion is, and vice versa. The room most often ignored by two Funs is a home office full of bills and other dreary tasks. Big surprise, right?

Problems with Organic Structures & Smart Structures

- They place a different emphasis on being on time than you do.
- They're too rigid about planning.
- They have more clutter than you.

Organic Structures and Smart Structures are similar to Classics about being on time, planning things, and written To-Do lists. Handle them the same way you'd handle a Classic. They'll be less annoyed with you if they're not in limbo. Organic Structures and Smart Structures are big-picture thinkers, so they're more patient than other planning types, but they have their limits.

Organic and Smart Structures have a harder time letting go of things than you do, so they accumulate more clutter. And you have a limit for what you can tolerate that's lower than theirs. You either deal with living with clutter, or you'll have to be the impetus for decluttering, which means it might not happen as much as you'd like.

Problems with Organic Freedoms & Smart Freedoms

- Their definition of "tidy" is quite different than yours.
- They can accumulate more clutter than you'd like.
- They leave cabinet doors open.

With these folks, you guys are the organized ones. Organic Freedoms and Smart Freedoms are more tolerant of mess than you, but they're not without redemption. They will take their marching orders to make you happy, as long as you keep them basic but specific. For example, a rule like "Shoes and coats go by the front door in bins or in your closet" is better than "Don't leave your shoes or coats strewn randomly around the house." The latter is basic, but not specific enough. Creating commonsense homes for items and clutter isn't second nature to them. One of Kelly's favorite quotes from her Organic Freedom sister Katie is: "As a kid, mom never taught us how to clean our rooms, so I never knew how to clean my room when she told us to do so. I'd just stuff it all in my closet or under my bed." Nobody taught Kelly either, but instinctively she knew how to create homes for things.

They also have more clutter than you, but they're motivated to attack it the same way as you: when it moves you, or when there's a deadline like a party. The other solution—and this is a luxury option to many—is to make sure they have a room or closet that they can keep however they want. No rules apply in this area, outside of their own whimsy. It's a great way for you to dump some of their stuff and close the door—although you'll eventually have to help them deal with the mess when it starts creeping out of the room/closet.

ORGANIC STRUCTURES & SMART STRUCTURES

You guys can live with most types because your organizational demands are flexible. You have minor issues with everyone but few big bugaboos.

Problems with Classics

- They hide things and contain them in ways that are not always practical.
- They mess with your piles.
- They're a little obsessive about trivial details and clear surfaces.

With Classics, you've just got to stand up for yourself and let them know what works for you. First, insist on visible storage options. They need to know that you can't have everything hidden away. When things are behind closed doors and in bins, you can forget about them if you're not accessing them frequently. Classics don't have a visual memory and know almost exactly where everything is in their house, especially if they created the system. Transparent bins behind closed doors are a good compromise; if bins are out in the open, you can have opaque bins, but then they absolutely must be labeled. Often you can get Classics to agree to transparent bins out in the open. At the end of the day, they want clutter and mess contained. It's why they'll combine a few piles into one big pile—something you can't stand. They're trying to minimize the mess. You need to have *your own* piles in labeled bins when living with Classics, or they'll mess with them even after you've pleaded with them not to.

You like clear surfaces too and have them where it makes sense. But you're also practical. Things need to reside on surfaces sometimes, and you like them out to remember and have easy access to them. Find out what surfaces absolutely have to be clear for your Classic. Hash out a workable compromise as to where you can leave things out in areas that are helpful for you. Classics also nitpick about your not immediately putting something back where it belongs. You like things to be done and tidy as well, but you know you'll get it done soon enough.

Problems with Funs

- They're frequently late.
- They plan things last-minute.

You really don't have too many problems with Funs. Sure, there's the occasional organizational detail that might be lost on you that isn't lost on them because they're detail-oriented. But these are minor skirmishes compared to your main problem with Funs, which is the way they manage time. They're often late to functions, and it drives you crazy. Be specific with them when it's really important that they be on time; and, if that doesn't work, lie to them about when an event will start. It usually takes them a while to figure this ploy out. As for last-minute planning, you've got to give them deadlines for when you need an answer regarding plans or making travel arrangements. Try your best to make it a real deadline, as in "Have it done by XYZ. I'm booking a flight that day, with or without your input," or "I'm RSVPing 'yes' on this date unless you object."

One place where you're on the same wavelength with Funs is the ebbs and flows of keeping a relatively tidy house. We say "relatively," because most of you are not exacting about a perfect house unless you had either a super-messy house or an insanely tidy house growing up.

Problems with Smart Structures & Organic Structures

- You have random disagreements over how some household tasks should be done and how much clutter you have.
- Organic Structures are going to have conflicts with Smart Structures over logic.

Strangely, you guys are going to accuse each other of having too much clutter, but you will have different reasons for having and keeping it. It will be strange, detailed things that annoy each of you, even if you're both Organic Structures or both Smart Structures. We have one Organic Structure client who is annoyed at the way her Smart Structure husband puts away the dishes. He has his logic for why he does it that way, and he's sticking to it. The only way anyone will convince a Smart Structure that there is a better way to do things is to show them or beat them logically in argument. You can also try the "If you hate the way it is, then you can move it back" tactic. Seeing is believing with both of you guys, so maybe your idea isn't as good as you thought it would be once you put it into action.

Smart Structures' trophies of various sorts—awards, books, etc.—might seem like meaningless clutter to others. However, Organic Structures are tolerant of clutter as long as it's tidy, so it rarely becomes an issue. Some of you who always close cupboard doors might find it odd if someone who is supposed to be similar to you leaves them open. You're not clones; you're just similar in how you like to structure your world.

Problems with Organic Freedoms & Smart Freedoms

- They actually have more clutter than you do.
- They are often late.
- They plan things last-minute.
- They don't keep things tidy as much as you'd like.

So, it seems like you have the most problems with these guys, but take a number: *everyone* has problems with them. They have trouble getting rid of clutter, especially items that have meaning behind them. Do as you do with your own clutter: schedule a time to attack it when it moves you, and do it with them. They also tend to pile things more than you do—if you can believe it—so try to get them on your transparent-bin bandwagon to put a little structure around their piles. Last but not least, Organic Freedoms and Smart Freedoms are, on the margin, messier than you'd like. Ideally, you give them broad but specific organizing rules and not too many of them: "Coats go on coat hooks, and shoes go under coat hooks," not "Hang up your coat, and put away your shoes." The latter isn't specific enough.

The other solution is to make sure they have a room or closet that they can keep however they want. No rules apply in this area, outside of their own whimsy. It's a great way for you to get some of their extra stuff out of your hair and then just close the door, as it's likely a mess.

Like Funs, their time-management skills are usually a bit wonky in terms of understanding what you can actually get done in ten minutes. These are the folks who call and say they're going to be ten minutes late and then show up half an hour later. So treat them the way you do Funs: double their time estimates. Organic Freedom Katie learned the hard way that only in the movies are weddings ever delayed. (She learned at her own wedding that the bride and bridegroom won't know you were late, or that you're leaving early, unless you tell them!) Organic Freedoms and Smart Freedoms can sometimes be quite thankful if you plan things ahead of time on their behalf. Obviously this means within reason; but when you make plans for them, it's one less decision for them to make.

ORGANIC FREEDOMS & SMART FREEDOMS

You guys can live with most types because your organizational demands are pretty basic. The trouble is that all other personality types are more high-maintenance to live with than you. Many of you are very specific about décor and aesthetics of even practical items, and that's where you need to stand your ground. One of the best solutions for you with all types is to make sure you have a room or a closet that's yours to keep as you please. It'll still be hard for some types to leave it alone, but maybe you can put a sign on the door that says "No Trespassing" to discourage nosy nellies.

Problems with Classics

- They hide things and contain them in ways that are not always practical.
- They mess with your piles.
- They're a little obsessive about trivial details and clear surfaces.
- They're always pushing their To-Do list.
- Things have to get done on their timeline.
- They're too rigid about planning.

Can you tell who is the most difficult for you to live with? It can be done, but you've got to be on your best behavior living with Classics; and, if you love them, obviously it's worth it. First, you must stand your ground when they're coming up with organizational systems. Make sure the things you need to remember are out and in view. Speak up and defend yourself if their organizing system isn't working for you. This is especially true when it comes to their touching your piles. They need to know that their idea of reorganizing your pile is your idea of completely messing up your organizational system. They'll scoff, but be adamant and get yourself those transparent bins and label them, even if one of the labels is "Hands Off!!"

Find out what their most important musts are. They're a little crazy about details in a way that doesn't naturally compute with you. Make those rules the absolute necessity, and follow the lesser rules when you remember or have the energy. With a Classic, the ideal solution is to have a space where you are free to be your shoes-off self, which is never as neat as a Classic, and be able to close the door on their judgment.

Problems with Funs

- Their definition of "tidy" is more exacting than yours.
- They have a lower tolerance for clutter.

Funs are just a lot tidier than you. They clean up messes when they see them and are practical about making sure the kitchen is clean. They use a plate for all food, and probably don't eat on the sofa at all. If you want harmony or sex, or to stop the yelling, you're going to have to channel the part of you that is the same as them, and that part is *time*. You guys are on the same page about time and will show up two hours early for a flight because you know how bad you are about time and don't want to be late. So harness that part of you that takes action when you feel like it, but think about how much that mess bugs your spouse more than you and take care of it when you see it. In fact, most of our maintenance tips for you are based on the ways Funs naturally stay organized, and that's to clean up the mess the minute it's made.

Problems with Organic Structures & Smart Structures

- Their definition of "tidy" is more exacting than yours.
- They have a lower tolerance for clutter.
- They're inflexible about planning.

You're both big-picture thinkers who don't notice the nitty-gritty of a messy room as much as other types. But Organic Structures and Smart Structures need more structure in their outer world than you do and therefore need a tidy house to truly relax. Organic Structures and Smart Structures can leave a dirty kitchen for a while, but not as long as you can. You can ask them what areas they like to be tidy daily, but you'll get a clearer picture if you just follow their lead and notice what they keep free of clutter.

Although you think you have the same level of clutter as these folks, they distinguish between their cherished objects and your clutter even if you can't. You can see why having your own room is so helpful; it keeps questions at bay. They're big-picture thinkers; so if you explain to them what's in process and the importance of certain objects, they'll usually understand. The key is to make sure you have proper homes for your clutter. It creates more order, and they'll be happier for it.

Organic Structures and Smart Structures are never going to be truly flexible about planning. If you have to change plans on them, drop the news on them and run. The reason you should run away is that if you don't, they'll likely take their annoyance out on you. But if you give them time to process it on their own, they'll have figured out a new plan that works with the change of plans and will have cooled down a bit.

Problems with Organic Freedoms & Smart Freedoms

- You disagree about random little things.

Just because you guys aren't the neatest personality types doesn't mean you don't have things you care about being kept nice. For example, Katie is obsessive about Christmas and has particular homes for each of her décor items and gets upset when others put them away wrong. It's almost a Classic trait to care that much about so many details. It's not something that every Organic Freedom is going to care about. It's these sorts of random things that'll throw you for a loop. The best you can do is to make sure on an ad hoc basis that the other person is aware of what's important to you, and why, and how to do it properly.

To prevent your home from devolving into chaos, maintain some basic, specific rules: coats go on the coat rack and shoes go in bins by the entryway, clean the kitchen once a day (ha, yes, there are people who do it more often), and go through mail every day. Then put each of you in charge of one or two of these basic rules so you might actually follow them. Obviously, all of our advice for your personality type will help, but these extra rules are just guardrails to keep you from going off the road.

CHAPTER FIFTEEN

Maintenance: I'm messy, or "OCD" and proud

Top Ten Obstacles to Staying Organized

1. Moving (Number one stressor for a reason: it's awful.)
2. Marriage/cohabitation (It's about more than the stuff.)
3. Remodeling (It's like moving three times.)
4. Divorce or breakups (Need we say why?)
5. Death of a loved one (Physical stuff, grieving . . . it's overwhelming.)
6. Children (At least eighteen years of constant organizational change.)
7. Health issues (Zaps you of energy.)
8. Financial difficulties (Ugh.)
9. Weather/seasons (It's annoying, but accept it, or move to California.)
10. Weight loss or gain (Only keep clothes that fit.)

So many of us are searching for the organizing Holy Grail—one perfect system that can forever grow with our life—that we keep an entire organizational industry in business. But it's a pipe dream. Life is a moving, growing, changing experience by definition, and so is organization.

When you're disorganized, there's usually one of the Big Ten reasons on the previous page throwing a wrench in the works; the reason quite a few of you look around your homes almost in defeat. Nearly all of these Big Ten have to do with change itself. Life's challenges take us all off guard at some point, no matter what your personality type; yet these obstacles will impact your organization (or lack thereof) in quite different ways and to varying degrees, depending on who you are. It is what it is. No shame, no blame. Acceptance is the first part of our PixieDust magic for a reason.

Moving

There is no harder or more stressful life experience than moving. Seriously. Google it. This is regardless of your type, because it involves a series of small, detailed, *and* big-picture moving parts. Think about it. Even if you were organized before you moved, you're going to have to pack up all your stuff into little boxes, deal with stairs, moving-truck mishaps, furniture that doesn't fit through small doors, figuring out what to tip movers; and finally, when you're done, you have to reorganize your *entire* household in a different space. Then throw in emotions, new neighbors, new routines, new dry cleaners, new everything, and you get why moving is considered worse than death—and that's pretty damn bad. If you have the money, then hire professionals who understand that it's your stuff, it's your life, and it's personal—organizers, movers, decorators, and so forth. Many of our repeat clients hire us just to manage moves. And if you don't have the money? Well, now you know why "Financial Difficulties" is on our Top Ten list. Moving without money sucks even more.

Once you're done with dorm rooms, it takes more than a day to move. Carve out enough time to unpack and organize if you can't handle the idea of living in limbo for a while—or hire someone to do it for you. We recently moved a Classic and a Fun with a two-year-old daughter from a small NYC two-bedroom apartment to a three-bedroom apartment a few blocks away. It took *seven days* with, on any given day, three to eight people working to finish this move properly. This was a NYC three-bedroom (i.e., small)!!

Marriage/cohabitation

Did you read Chapter 14: You're Driving Me Crazy! (page 202)? Yeah, this one is a doozy, especially if you have very different personality types. If you've ever seen the movie *When Harry Met Sally*, we are referring to the wagon-wheel coffee table. It's a minefield: moving; negotiating what stays, what goes; and the compromises involved. We won't even get into the closet-space issue.

Remodeling

A remodel is essentially three moves in one. Ugh. You have to create temporary organizational systems for goodness knows how long, as contractors tend to have personality types that don't accurately predict how long projects will take. Then, once it's done, you have to redo your organizational systems again. Most architects, contractors, and interior decorators rarely know as much about storage as organizers (e.g., having enough built-in file cabinets to hold your current filing needs, closets that fit your existing hanging garments, or—as was the recent case with our favorite client—a hidden, custom, pullout printer shelf that fits the printer in their library/office). Wait, do we sound like an ad for organizers?

Death of a loved one

This one is about emotional sadness and physical stuff. It's harder for some people than others, depending on type, but death is hard for everyone. This includes miscarriages, which often get shoved to the side by everyone but the mom-to-be. Even a pet's death can impact our ability to organize. Now, the double whammy is if death comes with dealing with that loved one's stuff. When this happens, you're dealing with a lot of the same issues as you did with cohabiting, except it's soul-crushing work. You've got to figure out what's worth keeping, what to do with it, what to sell; and for many types you've got to deal with guilt in getting rid of stuff you don't like. Get help, whether it's friends, local estate sellers, EBTH.com (an online estate seller) or 1-800-GOT-JUNK.

Divorce or breakups

This is another case of the emotional energy zap that can often feel like going through a death. It's also going to involve moving, possibly children having two homes, and reconfiguring all the organizational systems of our lives. Definitely no shame, no blame here. We'd suggest major purging. We don't know what it is about purging every square inch of your life after a breakup, but it opens up new doors. We have had quite a few clients in this situation who have hired us to clear them out; and almost inevitably, they've met someone new before we finished.

Children

First comes the baby, then comes the carriage . . . then the blankets, clothes, toys, stuffed animals; then it just multiplies from there. In fact, it was having children that got us into this business in the first place. Katie had always had trouble with organization, mostly her desk and her clothing; but once she added a baby to the fold, she couldn't keep up with the onslaught of stuff and mess. Children might be one of the hardest things to deal with organizationally, because their needs are constantly growing and changing.

Health issues

When you're sick, whether it's a physical or mental impediment, it makes it that much harder to stay organized even if you're already organized in the first place. In addition, medical stuff comes with loads of paperwork that can wreak havoc on your normal paperwork system. We had one client who had two folders almost six inches (15 cm) thick of old medical records from an issue he had. Often you're sick, dealing with annoying insurers, with no ability to find the physical energy required to keep your organizational systems in working order. This situation is a challenge for anybody.

Financial difficulties

We're sure many people have dealt with financial hardship over the last decade. When it happens, you feel out of control, zapped of energy and the ability to keep and stay organized. Keeping your kitchen organized might be the last thing you want to do, let alone the home office and all the bills piling up. But unlike uncertain financial times, your home, if you're not in danger of losing it, is a place that you *can* control and keep as tidy as possible, knowing it's okay if things get a *little* disorganized. Some types need to get their house in order before they can get their finances in order. Remember to focus most of your organizing energy on purging. Heck, sell some things and make some cash!

Weather/seasons

This one is pretty minor as far as life changes go, but it can be a major challenge for some personality types to deal with this constant change. We're talking about holiday decorations, hat-and-glove storage in the summer versus bicycle helmets and knee pads and swimming goggles in the winter. If you live in a place where the weather changes, maintenance is just that much harder.

Weight fluctuations

This is another minor, yet annoying and emotional, challenge that leads to overflowing clothes closets and drawers. It's hard to accept that your waist is never going to be that small again. It's only natural to hold on to clothes that no longer fit. Who in the heck wants to accept *that* life change? But once you let go, you will finally have an organized closet because you were brave and threw out everything that does not make you feel good about yourself or fit. Plus, letting go means even if you refuse to accept this life change—and you're working your tuchus off to get back into shape—you've opened the door for new, in-style clothes. Why do all that hard work just to wear your old clothes again?

Knowing your personality type and what parts of organizing are easy and hard for you is going to make it that much easier to overcome any of the Big Ten impediments. Stick to what's easy for your type. The easier it is to accept who you are, the easier it will be to maintain and tweak your systems as life continually marches onward.

CLASSIC STRUCTURES & CLASSIC FREEDOMS

Tips for Dealing with the Top Ten

1. **Moving:** Give yourself more time than you think you need to finish. Remember, you're not done until your décor is also done. Hire help if it's taking too long.
2. **Marriage/cohabitation:** Less is more. Purge and store whatever you can't get the other person to purge.
3. **Remodeling:** Create temporary systems that keep things hidden—the mess of a remodel will already be visually overwhelming—then try your best to pretend that you're an alien species and living in sawdust and disorder doesn't bother you. It'll be over soon.
4. **Divorce or breakups:** Need we say why these suck? Purge. It'll be cathartic.
5. **Death of a loved one:** If you truly can't deal, get a storage unit or equivalent, put everything in there, and wait. But you will feel better if you rip the Band-aid off sooner rather than later.
6. **Children:** You'll set up tons of great systems for your little critters; just know that you'll have more stuff than you prefer as long as you have kids living with you. Remember to plan for not only right now, but the not-so-distant future—the grand scheme.
7. **Health issues:** Try to let go of some of the less-important organizing details and routines. Ask for help, and accept that nobody is going to do it as well as you do.
8. **Financial difficulties:** Take charge of your life, purge, and organize things even if it means jerry-rigging until you can make organizational purchases. Dude, sell things and make some money.
9. **Weather/seasons:** Have a space carved out somewhere for off-season storage, both folding and hanging. It's a pain, but you'll love the extra space in your daily closet.
10. **Weight loss or gain:** Only keep clothes that fit. If ill-fitting clothes are inspirational, then keep the best one or two outfits and ditch the riffraff.

You're the champs of maintenance. As long as you have systems that work and you're not currently going through a Big Ten organizational wrench, then you're golden. But the minute there is a major upheaval that you were unprepared to face, it can start to feel like you're rearranging the deck chairs on the *Titanic*. Change is unsettling as it makes life feel out of your control; while technically this is always true, you appreciate when the façade is up.

The one thing you don't want to do in these situations is to give up on maintenance. For you, taking control of your surroundings is like therapy. It feels good and is why you're so good at maintenance! But when you're beyond overwhelmed, take a mental-health day or two before getting back to it—or hire someone to help you. Organizational therapy isn't as much about doing the straightening and organizing as it is enjoying it.

Finally, remember that your strengths are organizing, finishing things, being on time, attending to details, and planning ahead. You're not OCD: you keep the trains running on time! Use your powers to their fullest and remember to schedule some R&R throughout your week. Rome wasn't built in a day.

FUN FREEDOMS & FUN STRUCTURES

Tips for Dealing with the Top Ten

1. **Moving:** Give yourself a reasonable deadline to finish, like four or five weeks. Remember, you're not done until your décor is also done. If it's taking too long, schedule a housewarming party and hire help. One person didn't build your home, so why should one person finish setting it up?
2. **Marriage/cohabitation:** Purge, and store whatever you can't get the other person to purge. Less is more.
3. **Remodeling:** MacGyver whatever systems you need to survive this temporary hell.
4. **Divorce or breakups:** Need we say why these suck? Purge. It'll be cathartic.

5. **Death of a loved one:** If you truly can't deal—you're overcome with sadness—get a storage unit or equivalent, put everything in there, and wait. It's okay to grieve in your own way. You'll know when you're just procrastinating and it's time to tackle the issue.
6. **Children:** You'll set up tons of great systems for your kids. Remember to plan for not only right now but the not-so-distant future—the grand scheme. They will be gone someday, and life will be simpler.
7. **Health issues:** Ask for help and accept it. Even if it's not as good as how you do it, if it keeps things flowing, then go with it and let go of aggravations until you're better.
8. **Financial difficulties:** Take charge of your life, purge, sell things on eBay or Craigslist, and then organize. MacGyver things to your heart's content until you're able to make organizational purchases.
9. **Weather/seasons:** Whenever possible, have enough drawer and closet space so that you don't have to physically move seasonal stuff anywhere but the back of the closet or the bottom of the drawer.
10. **Weight loss or gain:** No grand plan here. If your closet is overflowing, fight your practical nature and get rid of clothes the minute you put them on and they don't fit anymore—or start that diet then and there. Don't overthink it.

Once you've got organizational systems that are working, maintenance is a snap for you. Even when it comes to change, you guys are the bomb. A crisis? You're the man/woman of the hour, especially extroverts. Your brain goes into a blue zone—neurologically speaking—and you can come up with solutions attending to minute detail on the fly faster than a Ferrari. The only trouble you encounter with maintaining organization is when you haven't installed big-picture organizational systems like we've suggested for you in this book (ha!) and some of your MacGyver solutions are making it hard to maintain things.

Our solutions for you in this book are designed to buttress your natural preferences for detail and help you stretch to look for the big picture and how your organizational needs might change, because once you've accepted that big picture, longer-term solutions are a better, more efficient way of doing things than one of your MacGyver plans; there's no looking back. You really won't need us again until, well, until you move.

ORGANIC STRUCTURES & SMART STRUCTURES

Tips for Dealing with the Top Ten

1. **Moving:** Use your big-picture planning skills and create a master plan with multiple To-Do lists prioritized to make the move run smoothly. Don't get too bogged down in the details. Keep moving forward.
2. **Marriage/cohabitation:** Come up with a plan before you actually move in together, as it will help you both communicate what's important and make the necessary purging feel easier and more sensible. Remember, less is more, and store what you have no room for but can't let go of . . . yet.
3. **Remodeling:** Set up new routines and systems so there is a semblance of structure amid the chaos. Dream of better days ahead. This too shall pass.
4. **Divorce or breakups:** Take on a ton of projects whenever you're dealing with this sort of devastation. It will keep your mind off of things, and the bonus is that you create some awesome stuff.
5. **Death of a loved one:** It's okay to put off the task of dealing with their stuff: just get a storage unit or equivalent so that it doesn't take over your daily living space. Take the time you need to grieve. Put the task on your Master To-Do list, and it will get done when you're emotionally ready.
6. **Children:** You'll set up tons of grand systems—some great, some so-so. Know that you'll have a little more stuff than even you like in your house as long as you have kids who live with you.
7. **Health issues:** Try your absolute best to let go of some of the less-important organizing details and routines. Ask for help and accept that nobody is going to do it as well as you do.

8. **Financial difficulties:** Create structure around you. It'll help you feel more in control and, in doing so, possibly help you come up with ideas to help get you out of your current situation.
9. **Weather/seasons:** Have a space carved out somewhere else for off-season storage, both folding and hanging. It's a pain, but you'll love the extra space in your closet.
10. **Weight loss or gain:** If your closet is overflowing and you can't bear to get rid of clothes that no longer fit, then at least store them someplace else until you're that size again or you accept reality.

The toughest Big-Ten life change for you is when you inherit new stuff en masse for whatever reason; then the basics fall short. But even without that kind of challenge, you will always have more stuff than other people. Accept it as a fact of life—keep it at bay with Later Boxes if need be—and move on.

Organic Structures, we've got an important side note for you: you don't have to keep gifts you don't like. Really. Life is too short to clutter your already-packed-full home with stuff you didn't choose and don't really want. Aunt Martha has been dead a long time, and she does not care whether her tea towel or figurines are in the attic, recycled, or sold on eBay.

ORGANIC FREEDOMS & SMART FREEDOMS

Tips for Dealing with the Top Ten

1. **Moving:** Ack . . . This is really, really, *really* hard for you because there are so many details involved. Hire someone to pack and unpack. If you've got no money, beg friends; offer food and booze. Intersperse boring tasks with fun tasks like hanging pictures and other décor stuff. It'll take a long time to get it right.
2. **Marriage/cohabitation:** This too will take a long time if you're in charge or married to someone like yourself. If not, let the other person take charge!

3. **Remodeling:** Luckily, you're better with change and staying in the moment, so channel that mantra as you're going through it, and save your energy for dreaming about what you're going to do when you move into the remodel.
4. **Divorce or breakups:** Use your penchant for staying in the moment and keep taking the next right step as you go through this difficult time. It sucks; go easy on yourself, but do your best to concentrate on a better future, and before you know it, you'll be living it. Dreaming is your jam; use it.
5. **Death of a loved one:** It's okay to put off the task of dealing with their stuff unless doing so helps you through the grieving process. If it's too much to deal with in the present, give yourself a break and deal with it when you're ready or can't afford the storage space anymore.
6. **Children:** It's an ongoing project, with more piles than you'll ever truly be able to keep up with. We know you'll keep trying, so use the same systems we suggest for yourself on your children. It won't always be this way, so do your best to stay ahead of their chaos and pat yourself on the back those few times a year when all their stuff is somewhat organized.
7. **Health issues:** Everyone needs help when they're not well, but you will need it . . . and then some. Your natural ability to put off onerous tasks can make disorganization pile up fast when you're not physically able to keep on it. No one is you, and it won't be as brilliant as you like it, but a floor you can see and walk through without stepping on junk is essential, even if the help messes with your piles.
8. **Financial difficulties:** Take it one day at a time, and use your ability to stay in the moment to your advantage. This too shall pass, and when you have the energy or large chunks of time, then take on the onerous task of details that so often accompany financial trouble and the actions needed to get out of it.

9. **Weather/seasons:** If you have the space, don't do seasonal change-outs, because sometimes you'll plain ol' forget you had a box of sweaters.
10. **Weight loss or gain:** Try to get in the habit of getting rid of clothes the moment they're stained or no longer fit. If you can't, then put them in a Later Box, or buy new clothes that fit to inspire you to ditch the old ones.

Hopefully, our book has helped you get to a place in your life where you can accept that you would rather be happy than perfectly organized. There are always going to be a few spaces that are a bit too messy and disorganized for your (or your spouse's) liking; but unless you're retired, we bet you just don't have the time you need to deal with it. You always have too much stuff, so actually any of those Big Ten can hit you hard. But the three life challenges that stand out the most among Organic Freedom and Smart Freedom clients as being extra troublesome are having children, being ill, and inheriting stuff.

With children, give yourself a big old break. Do your best and know it'll always seem more chaotic than the home of your friend who reminds you of Martha Stewart®. When your kids have fled the nest, you'll miss them and you'll see that when you're solo and you've got a well-planned organizational system in place, you're not as messy as you thought.

The second-toughest challenge to staying organized is illness, physical or mental, because it will 100 percent zap you of the energy to keep up with organization. Your lack of action with messes in this scenario will be misunderstood by other types who may be judgmental and think you're lazy. Tough. Life is too short to care about what other people think. Please take our advice to heart and make "No Shame, No Blame" your mantra. When you're able, you'll do what you can; when you can't, you know it's okay to take it easy.

As for inheriting other people's crap when they die—more stuff on top of your stuff and potential depression over their death? It's a veritable Bermuda Triangle for you. Give yourself more time than most to deal (get a cheap storage space for a few years if you don't have enough storage).

One Last *PixieTip!* for Everyone

Remember that magazine perfection is an illusion—it's a snapshot of one moment in time. It doesn't stay that way in the real world unless you have as much staff as the Earl of Grantham on Downton Abbey or the budget of Martha Stewart. Everyday beauty and perfection are in the eye of the beholder. Kelly's idea of neat will always be fundamentally different than Katie's. Kelly will always make her bed, because doing it makes her feel more in control and therefore relaxed and happy. Katie sometimes makes her bed—often right before she goes to bed—but she will never need to do it to feel relaxed and happy. At some point, if you stop listening to what other people tell you is—or isn't—"organized," you'll be able to stop searching for ways to better organize. Ask yourself: Do you know where things are, can you easily retrieve them, and can you maintain it this way? If you can, bravo. If not, set up (or rejigger) systems that work for you so that you can answer those three questions affirmatively for most areas of your home, and then just be yourself. Wouldn't that be nice for a change! Life should be easy, and the way to accomplish that is to organize your way.

APPENDIX

Organizational resources, room by room

Everyone has jumped on the organization bandwagon to the extent that even the furniture stores have organizational solutions these days. We've specified our favorite resources in the list below with a few special hard-to-find resources throughout the bulleted lists for each room. Use our phrases in the bullet points to help with your search so you can find what you need at every price point.

- Amazon®
- Anthropologie®
- Ballard Designs®
- CB2®
- The Container Store®
- Crate & Barrel®
- eBay®
- Etsy®
- Home Depot®
- Ikea®
- The Land of Nod®
- Lowe's®
- Overstock®
- Restoration Hardware®
- Serena & Lily®
- Staples®
- Target®
- West Elm®

Entryway

Matching coat hangers: Slender wood shirt hangers are best for all PixieTypes. For Smarts insistent on special hangers, mix in a few; just make sure they match the rest.

Accessory bins: You can find accessory bins at most of the retailers listed above, but don't forget that Smarts and Organics do better with acrylic, clear, or wire bins, and Classics and Funs do well with opaque bins. They can be lidded if you don't live with an Organic or a Smart. Also, consider Land of Nod—even though it's a children's store, it has bins that will work for all your rooms.

Bin labels: Classics and Funs should invest in label makers. Organics and Smarts should invest in tie-on labels or use clear packing tape to attach paper labels.

Double hang rods: These are great space creators for kids' coats.

Cubbyholes: You can either build them, or do a combination coat rack with a cubbyhole bench situated underneath. Or look for a mixture of similar options.

Coat racks: Check out coat hooks or standing coat racks.

Closet hooks: You can find utilitarian hooks easily via Google, or check out Etsy, Anthropologie, or Restoration Hardware for beautiful hooks. Make sure to coordinate the hooks' metal with any surrounding metal in your entryway, such as in doorknobs, tables, and the like.

Doormats: Natural fiber doormats or other unique options are available from Etsy.

Indoor/outdoor area rugs: Classics and Funs can find great area rugs from Dash & Albert®, but you can get cheaper alternatives elsewhere. Overstock is also a good source, and don't forget the rug pads!

Storage bench: These are useful for shoe storage. Shoe bins can go underneath.

Umbrella stands: Google to start your search, and go from there to find the perfect one.

Shoe bins: For Organics and Smarts, a couple of open, wire floor bins, or floor bins for the bottom of the closet work great.

Another shoe option for Classics and Funs are hanging shoe compartments.

Console tables: For Organics and Smarts, buy a multisurface console table for many piles and bins, or a console table with doors. Tables with hidden storage are best for Classics and Funs. All the furniture stores listed are good sources.

Mail trays: Get any beautiful tray at your preferred price point that looks great and holds your biggest mail items. For Organics and Smarts, acrylic, stacking letter holders or wire bins work well.

Wall bins: For Organics living with Funs or Classics, acrylic, wall-mounted magazine holders are great compromises for mail piles.

Key hooks: Do a simple Google search to find the perfect key hook, or look for a leather valet or bowl. Etsy is a great source (so is your china cabinet), and don't disregard high-end places like Tiffany's.

Home Office

Inboxes: The best inboxes for this space are on the larger side, so they can accommodate any size mail or package. They can be larger than what you might have in your front hall.

Desktop file organizers: We use both set and expandable folder desktop sorters to store files. Funs and Classics can use closed file boxes, but Organics and Smarts need open incline and accordion desktop file sorters.

Attractive file cabinets: If you're planning to go for basic metal cabinets, get an attractive color. If your office is in the kitchen, you can have a filing cabinet built into a lower cabinet. You can also buy file cabinets that look like furniture. Home Decorators Collection® is an inexpensive source.

Piling systems for Organics & Smarts: We suggest a few wall shelves around eye level, or an independent bookshelf. We like Sapien® bookshelves, but if they're not an option, console tables with shelves next to desks also work. Remember that stacked, shallow letter trays are only good for different printing papers—they make lousy bins for piling systems, as they nestle too tightly together to really pile properly.

Bins for Organics & Smarts: Wire letter trays are the best pile holders for Organics and Smarts. Large acrylic ones also work, but wire ones offer the most space so that your piles are not too tightly contained.

Drawer organizers: The Container Store always has the most reliable inventory of drawer organizers.

Bins for Classics & Funs: You can use lidded opaque letter boxes, as you can tuck away the lid underneath and keep them open or stack them if one pile is less used than another.

Attractive office supplies: Container Store always has good stuff, but if you really want to step it up a notch, check out www.seejanework.com or www.poppin.com.

Kitchen

Shelf risers: They're called "cabinet shelves" at The Container Store, which carries myriad sizes and styles.

Lazy Susans: We use ten-inch (25.5 cm), wooden lazy Susans for upper cabinets, but sometimes they can stick a little when turning. Plastic and stainless steel options work as well. Try to find lazy Susans without tall lips, as this limits wiggle room when storing items. Lazy Susans are musts for Organics and Smarts.

Pullout lower-cabinet drawers: Great in a pinch and often the right size, these require four screws to install. The customizable pullout shelves we've used are from a spot called Shelves That Slide. Don't forget to account for cabinet door hinges, as they take up about half an inch (13 mm) of space on each side.

Glass fridge containers: These are a great investment, because they go from fridge to oven to table.

Fridge bins: Help make the back recesses of your fridge accessible. Wide or divided bins work for all PixieTypes. Narrow ones are really only helpful for Classics and maybe a few Funs.

Knife blocks: Organics and Smarts do really well with magnet strips for knives as well as knife blocks without slots. In-drawer knife blocks are great for Classics and Funs looking to have one less item on their countertop.

Paper pads: Paper pads are not hard to find, and if you Google long enough, you'll find ones you like. But it's impossible to find pencils with magnets to stick to the fridge—Wellspring® is the only provider that sells them online. If you're not into paper, go ahead and get an old-fashioned whiteboard, or one of the new Boogie Boards®, and take a photo of lists before you head to the store. If you're technically savvy, there are tons of list and To-Do apps that you can find for your smartphone.

Garbage cans: We use pullout garbage cans from Simple Human®, as they are easy to install and they last. They require four screws.

Plastic-bag holders: We like to use Simple Human plastic-bag holders, which can be hidden inside cabinet doors, often under the sink. Or try the Urbano® Eco Trash Can to convert plastic bags into garbage bags.

Attractive kitty-litter storage: It's pricy but worth it. Try Modko® at www.modko.com.

Dining Room

Acrylic ghost dining chairs: Kartell® makes the original Louis ghost chairs, but these days there are a ton of other styles of ghost chairs as well as cheaper (yet still sturdy) versions.

Drop-leaf dining tables & other dining furniture: Every furniture store sells this stuff, but secondhand stores are a great source for attractive, inexpensive dining furniture of varying styles and older drop-leaf dining tables. Ditto for TV trays.

Replacement dishware, glassware, & flatware: Check out www.replacements.com before throwing your mismatched pieces out and starting afresh. Take your dining-room table settings up a notch with inexpensive, silver-plated flatware. eBay is a great resource.

Fix china: You can get epoxy glue designed for china to DIY, but it never looks good. There are experts everywhere who repair china and glass.

Hire an electrician to install your dimmer switch. Your local hardware store is a great resource for handymen, as is Craigslist. If you're thrifty and skilled, however, take a look at www.diynetwork.com.

Family & Living Rooms

Design tips: We're not designers, but we're good students, and we learned almost everything we suggest to clients about decorating from reading Lauri Ward's book, *Use What You Have Decorating.*

Pillow inserts: We found affordable pillow inserts at Pottery Barn. We know—go figure. They're feather, not down, but for a formal living room, you can't beat the price.

Mantel mount: You can get specialized TV mounts with heat-sensitive handles that help you pull them down to eye level so your neck doesn't crane.

Hiding wires: There are expensive, invasive wire-management solutions, and then there are anybody-can-do-it wire-management solutions. We love using 3M mini hooks to keep wires in place.

Attractive toys: If toys are going to be part of your living area, get attractive ones. Magic Cabin® is a great resource, as is Haba® products. Or you can always scour eBay for cool vintage ones.

Wall galleries: Our go-to suppliers for wall-gallery frames are either Pottery Barn or West Elm. They have the same parent company, Williams-Sonoma, so choose based on aesthetics and price.

Digitizing services: We're partial to www.ScanCafe.com for photos, but there are other digitizing services out there. Digitizing DVDs is a trickier business. Watch a YouTube® clip on how to do it if you're handy. For everyone else, find a college kid, or think your local computer-repair place (also, there's always Craigslist).

Photo organizers: Find someone in your area. We refer our NYC–based clients to a talented woman named Isabelle Dervaux. You can find her online at www.isabelledervaux.com.

Master Bedroom

Donations: We love this new site called DonateStuff, which helps you coordinate a pickup time with a local charity. Vietnam Veterans of America and the Salvation Army generally pick up donations, depending on where you live. As for drop-offs, you've got Goodwill and the Arc, plus countless local and regional charities—all of their websites delineate what they'll take and how—and don't forget those clothing-recycling dumpsters. As for nice work clothes, we're partial to Bottomless Closet® in NYC, which helps guide disadvantaged women into the workforce. Nationally, there's Dress for Success®. To make money off your good clothes, try Crossroads Trading®.

Huggable Hangers: Joy Mangano (played by Jennifer Lawrence in the movie *Joy*) created these great, thin, fuzzy hangers that prevent garments from slipping on and off. Huggable Hangers are perfect for all clothes except coats and suits. Pick black or ivory-colored hangers, as other colors don't stick around for long. Suit hangers are best because you can buy clips to convert them into pant or skirt hangers. You can get them at HSN® at www.HSN.com or The Container Store, as well as cheaper versions on the web.

Double hang: You can quickly turn any rod into a double hang at almost any home-goods store.

Closets: Elfa Closets at The Container Store are sturdy, long-lasting, and changeable, and you can put them up in any rental. When you're designing with them, know that their designers never maximize space—you can almost always fit in an extra shelf for shoes, because flats don't need a foot of space above them. Lowe's and Home Depot also have closet solutions—Rubbermaid® and Closet Maid®, respectively—but they're not as flexible and changeable as Elfa. All of these stores have higher-end closet designs similar to California Closets®, but, again, we're partial to Elfa, because as your needs change, you can alter the configuration without having to rip up the entire closet.

Izzy jewelry boxes from www.izzyjewelbox.com are perfect for Organics' and Smarts' jewelry that tarnishes.

Bulletin boards: We get attractive bulletin boards for jewelry from Etsy.

Clothing storage: If you lack storage space, there's a great service called Box Butler in NYC (or CityStash® in DC and San Francisco) that picks up and returns seasonal items on demand. And if you don't live in a crowded city and think you need a storage unit, then you have to purge!

Inexpensive feather pillows: Search for pillow inserts at Pottery Barn or The Company Store. Just double-bag them, which will give you a reason for holding on to stained and/or ugly pillowcases that don't match anything.

Bathroom

Chrome caddies for showers: Caddies are available from local hardware stores; Bed, Bath & Beyond®; Home Depot; etc. But if you want to hang a chrome caddy on a rental and are worried about damaging the tile, check out the clever German invention at www.nodrillingrequired.com.

Sliding shelves: You can get these at The Container Store or from Amazon, but Shelves That Slide are easy to install—check out the options on www.shelvesthatslide.com.

Opaque bins for toiletries: Any nonfabric bins will work. Opaque bins with some holes such as The Container Store's Like-It Bricks under-sink organizers are a great compromise when living with opposite PixieTypes.

Bathroom hook ideas: Command™ 3M hooks are great ways to put more hooks in a bathroom if you can't drill into tile, don't want them to be permanent, or have doors that are hollow or not thick enough. If you *can* mount into tile, don't forget to coordinate with the rest of your fixtures' metal.

Acrylic storage jars: These are perfect for Organics' and Smarts' cotton swabs and cotton balls. You don't need to keep the lids.

Toilet paper storage ideas: Enclosed toilet paper storage can work for Classics and Funs, while Organics and Smarts often do best with . . . surprise . . . open storage.

Toilet paper roll holders: These can be the standing kind, but something Classics might truly love is the bang for the buck of a combo toilet paper storage and roll holder. Interdesign™ makes for attractive storage. Our preferred method is to mount single post toilet paper roll holders on a wall.

Plunger storage ideas: If you're incredibly handy, there's this cool solution called the Hy-dit® kit that allows you to build a sort of mini closet to store a plunger, bathroom cleaners, etc. into the wall

Bathroom shelves: The lists of where to buy bathroom shelves are endless, but a few we use are listed at the beginning of the Appendix. You, or a handyman, can mount them anywhere unobtrusive (above the toilet is often a great spot) and at whatever heights suits the contents.

Medicine cabinets: Even if your home or apartment didn't come with a medicine cabinet, you can buy and mount them. They're worth it—even in a rental. No landlord will protest you spending your money to upgrade their bathroom. Some units even have a combination of open *and* closed storage—perfect for "multiple personality" households. Pun intended!

Hampers: Household Essentials® hanging hampers are a great space-saving solution in bathrooms.

Kids' Rooms & Playroom

Kids' hangers: The Slim-Line Huggable Hangers that work well for adults work miracles on kids' stuff, too.

Artwork storage solutions: Dynamic frames are a great way to feature artwork. There's also a neat app called Artkive®, where you take photos of work, enter the age of the child, archive it, and then order a book. They also offer a concierge service where you mail them all the work and they archive it for you and make a book. For those with excess artwork, large bins are the way to go.

Sentimental baskets: Sentimental baskets can be plain, plastic bins that are hidden away or underbed storage bins, but they can also be attractive ones on shelves. You can find them at any of the furniture sources listed on page 236.

Kids' bins: Most furniture retailers have caught on to the bin storage trend, and you can find attractive matching bins at the big ones. Pottery Barn, Land of Nod, and Restoration Hardware tend to keep the same kind of baskets in stock longer, which makes buying matching new ones that much easier if you run out.

Garage, Attic, & Other Storage Spaces

Shelving systems: Avoid plastic shelving, as it bows over time. Metal is the only way to go. Tall InterMetro® shelving at The Container Store or similar styles at Home Depot or Lowe's are our favorite. Put casters on them so you can move stuff around (just be sure to include two catty-corner interlocking casters to keep your storage from rolling off). Casters also raise storage solutions off the ground, which is great if you live in a flood-prone area. Remember, shelves can be placed at different heights to accommodate different bins. For garage walls, attics, and oddly shaped storage spaces, we favor Elfa customizable ventilated shelving at The Container Store.

Bins: Clear plastic bins of multiple sizes can be found at The Container Store. They're the best, and The Container Store rarely changes the stock.

Archival boxes: You can get archival boxes from other spots or online. But—big surprise—the ones we use are from The Container Store. Lineco® is the name of a brand.

Purge resources: Besides charities, check in the Master Bedroom section for donation resources (page 239).

Post-purge resources: Once you're in control of your cluttered storage and getting rid of only a couple of items at a time, you can sell items or give them away on Craigslist. We've found that local listservs are sometimes good bets, too. We have a friend who swears by www.freecycle.org. 1-800-GOT-JUNK is also a great resource when you can't deal with the charities; they don't just take everything to a landfill but recycle what they can.

Acknowledgments

This book was not made in a vacuum, although it certainly felt like it sometimes, especially in the midst of a particularly gnarly basement/storage/attic clean-out, so we would be remiss if we didn't acknowledge those who made the work worth it.

To all of our lovely clients, who were our patient guinea pigs and kept the PixieDust flying, but especially the amazing and delightful Daisy and Luc Dowling, whose homes we have organized and continue to organize, for being so excited about our concept and encouraging us in all our Pixie endeavors, it would not have been as much fun without you!

To our extended family and friends, who put up with our gossipy Pixie ways, letting us peek around your homes and answer questions about your living habits, as well as all that other fun family-and-friend stuff, and most especially for the laughter and hugs—we would not be or want to be who we are without you!

To our stubborn grandfather, John McMenamin, who showed us that even Classics can pile paper and how to live to be ninety-eight years old (and still counting).

To our brother and dad, who won awards for their Winston Churchill Thriller series—the ceremony allowed us to meet Gareth Esersky, who then became our persistent and infallible agent.

To our editing staff at Sterling Publishing—Barbara Berger, Kayla Overbey, and Melanie Madden—who deftly cut this whopper down to a lean-and-mean sampling of self-help. Also thanks to Chris Thompson, Wendy Ralphs, and David Ter-Avanesyan for their work on the interior and cover design.

To Lara Asher, who helped us come up with a better way to organize our book proposal, which ultimately led to Sterling.

To the ladies of theNYnetwork, who let us practice our rap and trade on you.

To Rebecca Perkins, whose Rouge Makeup Salons made us look ten years younger than we are for our author photo shoot and who thought our baby brother was worthy of her, even though his apartment was downright scary. We pixied the heck out of it, and, voilà—a business, marriage, and two kids were born (you're welcome, kid brother!).

To our dad for his terrifying red editor pen and our mom for her magical black artist's pen—we couldn't have done anything without you.

To six people who didn't exist when we first began percolating this idea—Dorothy, Meredith, Samantha, Edward, Charles, and William—thank you for continually making messes so that we were forced to come up with ideas to make life easier!

And, lastly, to Walter and Fred: You guys drive us crazy, but we love you anyway; our lives just wouldn't be our lives without you.

Thank you all!!

Index

Pixie Notes